Massage Ginny

Marvina Sims

ISBN: 978-1-957009-60-5 (sc)
ISBN: 978-1-957009-61-2 (e)

Library of Congress Control Number: 2022911812

LOVING IS NOT MY CHOICE

When I have to choose
I pick the one that's been loved the least
From the hurting human kind
to the stray battered beast!
It is when I have to love
I choose to love deeply
Actually...loving is not my choice
It's what chooses me.

LadyLottaluv

TAKE

IT TAKES
NOTHING
FROM YOU
TO BE LOVING
AND KIND
TO EVERYONE
EVEN
COMPLETE STRANGERS
BUT IT DOES
TAKE SOMETHING
FROM BOTH OF YOU
WHEN YOU ARE NOT
ACKNOWLEDGEMENT
AND KIND WORDS
CAN MAKE A DIFFERENCE
IN ENCOURAGING SOMEONE
TO LIVE A BETTER LIFE
AND EVEN GIVE THEM
THE DESIRE TO WANT
TO CONTINUE LIVING
I'VE LIVED LONG ENOUGH
TO KNOW
I WOULD MUCH RATHER
BE REMEMBERED
AS LOVING
AND KIND
THAN NOT
AND LIVE WITH REGRETS
I HOPE YOU
DO THOSE THINGS
THAT FEEL

OUT OF CHARACTER
BY SHOWING
SO MUCH MORE LOVE
NO LONGER
HOLDING BACK

SOMEONE IS
IN NEED OF
AND
LOOKING
FORWARD TO
YOUR LOVING
KINDNESS!

AGAINST MY WILL

I exited the elevator at the third floor. Although the sign says "INTENSIVE CARE UNIT" there are no arrows indicating which direction to go. The first two doors show, "Personnel Only" and "Do Not Enter" which is the one with yellow tape crossed in front of it. The third door is a sliding glass. On the wall next to it there is a metal loosely hanging with a symbol indicating wheelchair accessible, but it's so faded it's hard to tell where the silver metal ends, and the blue plate begins.

I hit the metal plate. As the double sliding doors open extremely slowly it screeches like an old, rickety, wooden roller coaster along a rusty track. I push myself into room two, where my aunt Mira is sleeping. They finally took all the tubes from her arms and nose. I look up and see an old television show playing in black and white. I don't bother to remove my coat figuring if she doesn't wake up in ten minutes, I'll just write a note and leave.

She told me over the phone that she had just had the temporary pacemaker surgically removed. It is no longer needed since she finally agreed to start dialysis. The toxins had gotten so bad in her system it caused her heart rate to slow down. She's had her first dialysis and all of her vitals are back to normal, which is why her pacemaker has been removed only three days after it was put in.

I hear a bell chime. I look at my aunt, Mira, thinking maybe it came from somewhere around her. Her eyes pop open. "Ah!" she yells. I can't tell if she's excited to see me or if I scared her. I laugh. She starts laughing. The bell rings again. We look at each other. She says, "That ain't me." I look at my phone. It's the notification from my front door camera app. Another squirrel is scampering along my front porch. I watch it until it jumps onto my neighbor's porch then disappears from the camera's view. I put my phone away.

"Have you been allowed to eat again, yet?" I ask her.

"Yeah, but I don't want that nasty junk," she says.

I chuckle. Then a spot on her neck grabs my attention. “What did they do to your neck? It looks like a quarter is sticking out of an open slit. And they just threw clear plastic tape over it.” I take a picture and show it to her.

“I don’t know what they’re doing to me. Baby girl was up here yesterday getting on their asses ‘cause the nurse put the needle in my arm wrong and caused it to swell up.”

I raise my eyebrows. “Yeah this place gives me the creeps. I didn’t like how they cared for Mama when she was in here. Getting off the elevator it looks like an abandoned building. I didn’t know which way to go to get to *your* room.”

My stick-on visitor’s pass falls into my lap. I bawl it up and throw it into the trash next to the bed stand as I ask, “Did they say when you’ll be getting discharged?”

“They’re saying possibly tomorrow but I’m ready to get the hell outta here now.”

We get quiet to watch snippets of the black and white tv show, Bonanza[1], but once the commercial comes on, I tell her, “I’m gonna be heading on home.” I stand on my footrest to kiss her goodbye.” She thanks me for coming to see her.

I go back through the double glass doors. I thought the elevator was to the left but now I don’t even see it. I push open another door. Still no elevator.

I turn around to head back when a man dressed in a white uniform opens the door. He looks shocked. “Whoa…sorry…Are you lost?” he asks.

I tell him, “I’m looking for the elevators.”

He asks, “Where are you trying to go?”

“To the parking lot,” I reply.

He looks at me questionably and asks, “Have you been discharged?” I roll my eyes in my head because I saw him looking at my wheelchair. Now he’s assuming I’m a patient. “I cannot get discharged if I was never a patient!” I snap.

I continue pushing myself through the door. He grabs the handle on the back of my wheelchair. Stopping me abruptly almost making me topple out of my chair. But I push my body back just in time.

With gritted teeth he says, “Before I let you go, I’m gonna need to check our system to make sure you’re supposed to be leaving.”

I yell. “Let my chair go! I’m not a patient here! I was visiting my aunt!”

He continues pushing me in a direction as I’m holding the wheels trying to stop him.

“STOP...Got damnit!” I scream.

I lock the brakes, but he continues pushing. I continue ranting. “I Just told yo’ ass I don’t belong here!” I grab the wheels. He tilts the chair upward so that the front wheels are able to continue gliding. I can’t stop the chair from rolling now.

I start screaming. No one comes out. I grab the side rail on a hospital bed, which is lined against the wall. He continues pushing. My body is yanked from my chair and I hit the floor. I quickly scoot toward a door.

He grabs the hood of my coat and creepily whispers, “Why are you insisting on making this more difficult than it has to be?”

I yell. “HEEEEELP! HEEEEELP!”

He stoops down. Looks directly into my eyes, with his blood shot red eyes and whispers, “Something tells me you were trying to escape our psych ward.”

I begin crying and yelling. “I don’t fucking belong anywhere near here. Why da fuck won’t you listen to me? I was going...”

He interrupts, “Good night...You crippled psycho bitch!”

---

1 *Bonanza* is an American western television series that ran on NBC from 1959 to 1973. (Wikipedia)

THEM WORDS

Ox becomes ax
Was could be wax
Shot becomes shit
Ship equals shop
We post the past
Or past the post
Then get the got
Making man mad
Creating med men
Sand becomes sane
And brain turned drain
Making a massage into a message
Pronunciations become messy
Would you prefer more or mores
Did you read or have you read
Would you rather go live or just live
To lead is good but lead is poisonous
We can even eat a desert in place of a dessert

A slip of a tongue can be fun
But one incorrect slip of a character then you better
Not sign that dotted line

15 could slip into 25 years
10 more years of misery for a homeowner or a prisoner
yet miraculous for the fatally ill
$500000 made $50000
equals falling short in assets
or lessening a debt
11.2% dislocated decimal 112%
a personal loan turned into a life sentence

It's not only how you say it but how you write it
If communication is the key what does it unlock
Gratification or misery

- ✓ *In direct* is straight forward, towards somewhere or someone without stopping or changing direction: a direct route/line.
- ✓ *Indirect* is round about, not directly; Indirect sunlight doesn't shine right on you – it reflects off a window.

Can we indirectly love someone
What does indirect love look like
Is it more doing without saying

When someone says, "love you" isn't that
indirectly, since the "I" is left out
Do you still hear it directly
Or did it bounce in different directions like a
reflection in seven separate mirrors

Words most often make no sense. And too
often get interpreted totally wrong
We put too much emphasis on words
Too little prominence on emotional energy and sound
Proceed with caution with
them words!

JANBILACAL

Sink holes are a new irregular galaxy, similar to irritable bowel syndrome, resembling ovulation discomforts. Gigantic wombs times 500,000. A vagina in reverse because you can go in but you'll never come out the way babies, blood and secretion can. Vagina is so yesteryear. Janbilacal—a better-quality umbilical cord—is the new earth.

Don't just stand there.

Jump in!

Welcome!

You are pap smearing through Janbilacal. But first as a side note: If you slipped into that medium sized crack that was big enough to let you in because it was newly formed, and you didn't see it while going about your daily routine, or if it suddenly opened wide enough to swallow your entire house and garage and you were in one of them, or if you were sitting in your car in traffic, or you were walking your dog, or if someone unexpectedly pushed you in, or held your hand as they jumped, pulling you in unexpectedly, then the rest of this message is not for you.

Be proud of yourself because you have just taken part in the first and last penetration of a new dikless world. I must apologize because we are well aware that that final jump is likened to revisiting your throbbing, popped cherry, upon exiting virgin hood. I'm pretty sure while on your way down, you desperately reached out, in hopes of clinching at anything you could to avoid a deadly impact. Kind of like how a drowning person would grasp at a straw, as if it were a floaty to save their life, regardless of how unproductive it was.

It would have been a great benefit to you, as you were falling in, if you were able to grab and store all the dirt you could handle, as this has done two things to benefit you: 1) create more weight which helped you to literally hit rock bottom much faster, 2) will help you form quality polyps, also known as dirtballs, that you'll need for building your own new miniature Janbiliacal.

Our goal is to be just like snowflakes. Well...Wait...Not literally, of course. Who would actually go around dreaming of having those type of horrendous, multi-two-dimensional shapings of confusion, relying solely on temperature and humidity for formation, only to have a one-second lifespan, upon hitting a surface?

I guarantee you anything close to resembling what you once called a family, as in looking and acting exactly alike, can be worse than what you once called karma. Therefore, we highly discourage it. In Janbilacal we are all higher Jans. What you once referred to as:

God
Allah
Jehovah
The Universe
Homes
Cars
Higher Education
Jobs
Cigarettes
Gambling
Cannabis
Alcohol
Husband/Wife
Wife/Wife
Husband/Husband
Child
Cat
Dog
Sexual Pleasures
Money
Or the Almighty Grub...
No longer exists here.

We're going to take a detour now.

Please do not be alarmed by the glop you are treading. That is the substance needed to build your higher character. That is if you plan to ever leave here at any time. On earth you refer to it as shyt, as in "shyt happens." We call it rung. In order to be a "Higher Rung" you must endure seven layers of it:

Dung
Crap
Feces
Manure
Poop
Bull pies
and then your final rung of
Meadow Muffins.

Notice the various colors, smells and textures. Shocking aromas, huh! So pungent, as if it is already on your tongue...Mmmm. All flavors are non-discriminant, of course. That's just to remind you that all layers of shyt is good for you in the long "rung."

It's your turn to create your desired polyps or dirt balls, as pretty or as hideous as you desire. Smart azz and dumb fuks are also options. But don't make too many of any of these or you will have to celebrate their dirt days eternally. Keep in mind you are ruler over your own creations. So, if you are easily, highly irritated by dumb questions, clingers, and moochers...

DON'T CREATE ANY.

Good news! Gone are the days of dysfunktional families. Well, actually this is not as good as it may sound right now. We would be bored shytless if there weren't any prostitutes and pimps, drunks and druggies or shows like Cheaters and 48 hours to arouse our excitement about other peoples screwed up lives.

Embrace your dirtfunktional mud balls because that's what they turn into every time your tears spill out over all the warnings you give in an attempt to save their pathetic lives. Yet they continue doing dumb shyt anyway, causing you and everything affiliated with them to fall into the next level Janbilacal—the Retral-birth—which is a lot worse than what you call hell.

Oh wait! What am I saying? The higher rung actually leads to a hellish retral-birth!

BRYKED

"Maaan...I don't know why you don't believe me. I didn't take yo shit." Bryk's words are slurred. Strapped to a wrought iron chair, his chin is pressed against his chest as blood oozes from his mouth and trickles down his forehead, into his left eye.

Snake kneels into a frog position to become eye level with him. "Now Bryk you know damn well...all you had to do was ask me for ANYTHING...and it was yours. You *neva* had to steal SHIT, from me. You had *er'thang* you needed and even a lotta shit you'll never *use* let alone *want*. So, I don't know whatchu felt you had to prove."

Snake shakes his head, looking down at the concrete basement floor, as he slowly rises to stand. He looks at the other three guys, standing around. Glancing over the brick walls, he spots a crumbling brick, and mumbles to himself, "I really need to get that fixed....Hey Big Shedy!"

Big Shedy jerks his head in Snake's direction. Snake pulls a pillowcase, from a pillow that is lying on a cot. "Go fill this up with at least six loose bricks...from *outside* 'cause I know yo' dumb ass would try to get them off the walls in here." Snake raises his eyebrows before asking, "Now, how many did I say get?"

Big Shedy raises his eyebrows. "Six," he replies. He takes the pillowcase. Being overweight and the pain in his hip causes him to wobble toward the door.

Snake emphasizes, "No more and nothing less...A'ight?"

Big Shedy nods, closing the door behind him.

Rock shakes his head, as he watches Big Shedy leave. "Dat nigga sho needs to lose at least two hunerd pounds fo his ass die, just tryna walk. I betcha if his ass ends up in da penitentiary, he won't have no problems 'cause da way dat nigga love to eat fat, greasy meat, biscuits, beans, bacon and burritos, dat mufuka gone prefer starvin' when he see what dae serve in dat mufuka."

Snake snaps. "Damn man! Yo fuckin answer to er' problem is da fuckin penitentiary!"

Rock cuts his eyes at Snake and snaps back. "Yeah well I should know since I did time fa yo ungrateful ass! See if that shit eva happens again tho! So, you bet not fuck nutin else up."

Snake bawls up his fists. Presses his forehead up against Rock's, speaking between grinding teeth. "Whatchu threatenin' me now mufuka? Let's just say right about now is when you get tired a throwin this bullshit back up in my face...Ya feel me?" They continue staring each other in the eyes before Rock finally slowly backs up.

Streng, who is hearing impaired, looks each man in the face, trying to make out what their conversation is about. He knows not to ask, knowing they get pissed when questions are asked, especially Snake. So, Streng makes do with whatever lip reading he can catch. When it looks as if everyone finally stops moving their mouths, he breaks in. "Yall see the Bulls game last night?"

Snake reacts, waving both hands in the air. "Maaaan don't bring they *BOOOL* shit playin' back up! Gon' make me mad all ova again."

Streng bursts out laughing. Then looks at Rock and says, "Man, dat wasn't nobody's fault but yo flamin', faggoty ass boy, Dennis Rodman. If dat mufuka was more interested in winning than he was with havin' a rainbow ass, hair fashion show, dae woulda took da game."

Rock bursts out laughing and yells, "Rodman wasn't in that by hisself! Don't put all those fucked up plays back on my, man!"

Streng replies back, "Look atchu...takin' up fa yo amazon ass hairy bitch." He flicks his wrist and rapidly blinks his eyes.

The door flies open. All eyes shift to Big Shedy as he wobbles back inside. "Maaan I had to walk all da way up to California and Madison, to get dese from dat vacant lot. Yall know where dae tore down Ray's liquor store...found me a $20 bill in dat mufuka too."

Snake snatches the pillowcase full of bricks. "Dude! Like I give a fuck!"

Rock's forehead crinkles as he glares at Big Shedy. "Damn dude... You sweatin' like it's a hunerd degrees out dere, and it's only like twenty-five tho." Rock shakes his head in disgust.

Snake slowly walks over to Bryk, wrapping the open end of the pillow case around his hand. "As much as I love you, nephew. You showed no love in return...so this is the consequences. I really hate you had to go there with me, but you need to know fuckin over me is not an option. Not in this lifetime."

Snake swings the pillow case a couple of times before bringing it down on top of Bryk's head. It jerks back and dangles to one side, along the back of the chair. Snake swings again and another blow lands on his face. Then a third time on his chest. Blood gushes from Bryk's mouth and oozes from his nose.

Snake drops the bag of bricks to the floor, as tears trickle down his cheeks. Speaking softly, he says, "Clean dis shit up."

Streng, Rock, and Big Shedy each take their positions of cleaning the blood from the floor and walls. As Streng and Rock lie Bryk's body on plastic and roll him inside, Big Shedy is in the backyard nailing eight-foot-long, two-by-four boards together. He has two sides of four boards nailed, creating an L shape, when Streng and Rock carries Bryk's body out. Big Shedy steps back as they toss the body down on one side.

Rock snaps, "Maaaan this all you did! You know dis big nigga's body gone need at least seven boards nailed together, if not more, just to cover his back side...Give me that damn hammer!" Snatching the hammer, Rock looks around the ground frantically and asks, "Where da fuck da nails at!"

Streng spots them and hands one to Rock. Rock hammers so fast it sounds like a woodpecker's pecking a tree branch.

Once he's finished, the body is enclosed in a square, wooden fence-like, coffin.

Big Shedy scrunches his face then says, "Man, you need to figure out how to cover the bottom and top cause if the cops pull us over..."

Rock turns swiftly, raising his hand in the air, as if he is about to back-hand slap Big Shedy. Big Shedy cowers. Rock gets in his face, spitting as he speaks. "Don'tchu fuckin' jinx us with that bullshit talk!" Rock backs away as Big Shedy wipes the spit from his face.

Snake steps outside and shouts, "Let's go turds! Time is..."

Rock interrupts. "Slow up, Snake. We have to cut about a foot off some boards to cover his head and feet."

Snake grits his teeth, "Well if we wait long enough, his rotting body will give itself away, so hiding his ass will be a waste. Now, won't it?"

Rock knew not to respond, as this would have infuriated Snake more.

Snake then yells, "Hurree da fuck up...gotdamnit!" He storms back inside.

As Streng evenly saws twelve inches from more boards, he hands it to Big Shedy, who smears it with glue, and hands it to Rock, who stacks each one inside the open hole of the makeshift coffin. The head is completely hidden, and only a few more boards are needed to enclose the feet.

Streng thinks to himself once each end is closed in, no one will know the head from the feet. He starts to write the word "top" over the head. He finishes the "T" but stops. Figuring it really doesn't matter anymore now.

Rock and Big Shedy, hear a car engine approaching as the tires make a crunching sound over the fragmented concrete. They stop working to look toward the gate, near the alley. Once the headlights are in view, Streng finally looks up from sawing. The driver stops. The window slowly lowers, as a lot of smoke comes out it looks as if the inside is on fire. A man speaks, "Where Snake?"

Big Shedy yells out, "Wrong address!"

The driver laughs maniacally, then drives away. They look at each other and get back to work.

Rock glues the last piece. "That's it yall." He proudly states. He wipes his hands on his pants and proclaims. "Oh shit...we forgot to put the straps around it, so it'll look like a bundle of loose two-by-fours being held together, like at Home Depot."

Streng adds his idea. "Well then we gone have to do two more bundles like that."

Big Shedy jumps in. "Only 'bout two more and that's it, 'cause we don't want too much weight in that pick up." He wobbles into the basement to get Snake.

They all lift the body onto the back of the pickup truck. Since it is dark and to avoid drawing too much attention on the bigger streets, Rock drives along side streets for as long as possible, doing rolling stops at the stop signs. When they come to the end of a block where the only option is to turn right or left, Rock looks at Snake, who is sitting in the passenger seat and asks, "Which way now?"

Snake hesitates before responding. "Head to Lake Street."

Rock turns right. Lights begin flashing behind them.

Snake mutters under his breath. "Aw shit!" Then looks at Rock. "Did you have the turn signal on?"

Rock gets irritated. "Yeah man."

Snake snaps. "Don't fuck this up man."

Rock snaps back. "Have I eva...fa you?" He pulls over.

Streng begins slicing his fingertips with a razor blade, in case they have to go to jail. He already has enough prison records. He purposely left his ID at home. If they get arrested, he'll give them a fake name. He's already decided to use his brother's name since he never paid him his money back. He's hoping he fucked up his fingertips good enough, so the fingerprints won't match any of his previous records. He snatches his black wash cloth from his back pocket and squeezes it so that the blood would stop trickling. He passes the razor blade to Big Sheddy. Big Sheddy holds the razor between his fingers.

The police officer walks up to the truck and flashes his bright flashlight in the back seat first. Once the officer positions the light towards the driver, Big Sheddy shoves the razor into his shoe.

Rock rolls the window down. The police officer tells him, "Turn off the ignition. I need to see your license and insurance." He flashes the light into Snake's face. Then the back seat again.

Rock asks, "What's the problem officer?"

The officer snaps. "I'll tell you that once we're better acquainted. Now slowly hand over your information."

The second officer, who is standing on the passenger side is fidgety and looking around. Rock moves extremely slowly as he leans toward the glove compartment.

The officer gets irritated. "Oh, you wanna fuck wit me now?!"

Rock stops in mid lean. “No sir, officer. You said slow and I don’t want nooo misunderstanding.”

The officer asks, “You gotta gun in there or something?” He doesn’t wait for an answer when he snatches his gun from his holster.

Officer number two does the same.

Everyone in the vehicle starts yelling at once.

“Whoa!” Rock yells.

“Holon now!” Snake yells.

“What da fuck!” Streng yells.

“Aw hell naw!” Big Shedy yells.

The officer yells. “Slowly step outta the vehicle. Sit on the curb in front of the truck. Leave the headlights on. Each of you spread out…arm length!”

As they position themselves along the curb, officer two radios in. “We’re gonna need back up.”

Looking back at the officer, Snake interjects. “Officer there’s no need for backup. We’re just working on making some repairs to my mom’s house. We were on our way…”

“Shut da fuck up!” The first officer screams.

While officer two searches the truck, officer one looks down at Streng. “Why is there blood on your fingers?” Streng doesn’t answer and looks at Snake for clarity.

Snake speaks up. “He’s hearing-impaired sir.”

The officer turns to Snake. “You better not be bullshittin’ me.”

He then walks right up to Streng and stands on his shoes. Streng looks up at the officer confused. Then looks at Snake again.

Snake overexerts his mouth movement as he explains. “He asked about the blood on your hands.”

Streng responds. “Oh, sorry ocifer. I dient hear chu. I cut m’sef’ sawin’ woo’.”

Snake shakes his head as he lowers it to hide his smirk at how Streng loves lying, acting and talking extra dumb, especially if he thinks it’ll keep his ass out of trouble.

Three more police cars pull up. More flashing lights. They all huddle around chatting. Their radios blare in and out with police jargon. One of them, seeing the pick-up truck doors open ask, “Was there anything in the truck?" The first officer turns to face him as they begin mumbling.

The first officer walks back toward Snake and asks. "So, what's with all those two by fours stacked on the back of the truck?"

As Snake is about to answer shots ring out. Everybody ducks and dive to the ground, except the first officer who is still standing. But then falls flat on his face between Snake and Streng. Blood oozes from underneath the officer's body.

The book *Duplex Occurrence* was originated from this short story. You can purchase *Duplex Occurrence* from www.MarvinaSims.com, Amazon and Barnes and Noble.

BOUNDARIES

For those who are unaware boundaries are mandatory to maintain a sense of self-love and confidence so that enmeshment is avoided. BOUNDARIES are too often ignored by those who do not mind violating your space.

It is not safe to Believe
Others
Understand
No **D**iscretions
Are **R**equired
In **E**very **S**ituation.

An obligatory invisible dividing line from state to country, wall to room, physical location. Equally and especially important for givers and takers, pourers and drainers, emotionally exhausting vampires.

You are not aware this is a thing until you are physically tired from doing absolutely no-thing.

Suffering psychosomatically. Severe migraines appear then disappear without a sensible explanation.

IT IS NOT OKAY
To say yes when you really mean no
To interrupt your plans to cater to someone else's
To sacrifice your time to go when you need to rest
To go along with immorality making you uncomfortable
To smile when you want to cry-going along to get along.

IT IS OKAY
to not be okay
To make loving yourself a priority
To value yourself and demand respect
To not be concerned about how others view you
To live your life as you desire for your own happiness
To reset all **BOUNDARIES** if all others bomb

If hitting the reset button miscarries, distancing is the new reboot.
Realigning into a healthier location.

No longer a dumping ground for other's:
Pessimism,
Lack of enthusiasm,
Misdirected anger,
Sick self-esteem.

It is delusional to believe that a violator's behavior will cease based on your desire for it to be.

Shelter your:
self-love, health, trust, happiness, laughter,
peace, energy, mind, creativity, identity.

Build your own:
walls, partitions, barriers, dividers, separators,

BUILD BOUNDARIES TO PROTECT YOUR SPACE!

SPIRITUAL CONNECTIONS

Food makes for great conversations

It's spiritual

I believe it to be so

Every time I prepare certain meals

I think of deceased loved ones

A warm feeling due to food

Fond memories

And Close connections

I finally understand why *Day of the Dead* is a thing

The Hispanic culture comprehended the connection 3,000 years ago

RATATARIAN WIGWAM

Every generation of Verodens are born homeless. Their only means of continuity is stealing–discarded laems, heat during winter, and cool air during sweltering summer months. Droughts are not a thing. As long as rainy days return, sewers continue to overflow.

As a matter of fact, most Verodens are satisfied with secretly scrounging outdoors for even the tiniest bit of laems, which is tossed out from the Bumeebles, who live great lives of luxury, and think nothing twice of wasting laems.

There are two Verodens, Squish and Squash, who have big dreams and desire to live as Bumeebles. They break into a quiet cradle, where a family of Bumeebles are expected to be sleeping. But one Bumeeble, Nana Pa, lies awake in the moonless blackness.

She hears the pittering claws along the plastic walls and across the glass floors. Thinking she's imagining things she finally drifts off to sleep. But is soon awakened again by the loud crunching of the pet sloth's scum. She looks up to see the sloth is still dangling from her mugwort. This is confirmation that some other invertebrate is lurking.

As Nana Pa climbs down from her smudge bundle, the crunching stops. She figures the best way to catch the invertebrate is to morph into a sloth scum.

A few neonates later, Squish and Squash return to finish the delectable sloth scum. Just as they are about to take a nibble, Nana Pa unmorphs, gripping them by their miniature husks, and tying them both together with a slither of the smudge bundle. Using the smudge bundle as a tie automatically sends a signal to the invertebrate brutes.

The brutes arrive within nano-neonates, snatching Squish and Squash off to an offshore Ratatarian enclave. There are thousands of Verodens here, endlessly pittering and sniffing, in search of laems.

Heading the Ratatarian is Arch Veroden, Skrodum Cartilage. He wastes no neonates getting started. “Listen up yous…sewer luvin, moth ball deodorant wearin, Bumeeble wannabees! Take a look around you! You are *all still* Verodens! Say hello to your cousins, and your cousins, cousins. Yo mammy and grandmammy are probably around here as well.

You’re here wasting all of our neonates merely because you actually thought you could break into a Bumeeble’s cradle and nibble yourselves into becoming an actual Bumeeble! HAHAHA-HAAAA… How’s that workin for ya?!

Welcome to my nowhere-near-Bumeeble-like acropolis, The Ratatarian Wigwam!

DISTANCE

Even in the distance I can hear
the sun screaming
the moon laughing
the stars singing
the galaxy mating

Even in the distance I can smell
the lava boiling
the water and soil coagulating
the precipitation brewing
the roots intertwining

Even in the distance I can feel
the earth rebirthing
the wind wandering
the sky churning
the perennials pollinating

Even in the distance I can taste
the extinction of rabbits
the carcasses decomposing
the oozing fungus
the grass bulldozing through concrete

Even in the distance I can see
the hunt for prey
the trickling o-positive blood stains
the clotting veins akin to tree roots
the fatal de-circulation of a vascular system

Even in the distance I can sense
the reciprocity of a fetus
the nipple lactating
the infant latching
the soul wrenching end re-dwelling into eternity.

SEVERELY INTERRUPTED

Female characters:	Vanity
	Moné
Male character:	Unknown stranger
Voice Over:	Restaurant host
Voice Over:	Gorilla scream
Setting:	Vanity and Moné are Downtown in Chicago. They go inside the Rain Forest Café restaurant to reserve a table for two. They order cocktails, return outside to sit on a bench and wait for the host to call their names.

Voice Over: Gorilla screams

Vanity: I survived my yearly gyne exam today.

Moné: Good for you. Another yeast infection?

Vanity: That was so last year. This year I'm too dry. After my doctor is done tickling my tits and digging and poking all inside me, she asks, (mocking in a high nasal pitch) "You're not feeling any irritation down there?" I told her I figured it was just strands of dog fur scratching me. I mean the dog *is* shedding and I *do* sleep naked. Simple logic. Right?

Moné: So, what's the prescription for that?

Vanity: At first, she suggests I buy an over-the-counter lubricant-KY jelly. But then she changes her mind and says, "Better yet let me write you a prescription for a cream."

Moné/Vanity (in unison): Of course, she does! (laugh)

Voice Over: Gorilla screams

Vanity: I get to the drive through pharmacy to pick up the cream and the pharmacist semi yells seventy-five dollars and seventy-six cents. Under my breath, I'm like, for a tube of cream? What the fuck! So, I repeated it and ask, seventy-five dollars and seventy-six cents, to make sure I heard her correctly. She repeats it, yes seventy-five dollars and seventy-six cents. I'm sitting, debating with myself. Thinking this coochie cream gots to be extremely potent. She gets impatient and asks, "So do you want it or not?" I go ahead and hand her my debit card. Do you know when I gets home and read over the receipt and prescription, I notice the price is only five dollars and seventy-six cents? I'm like what type of fragernackle bullshit just happened. And I hadn't even smoked yet. So then, I read the usage for the cream and it says only use externally. Do not use on eyes, ears, mouth or vagina. Can you believe that bullshit? Who does that? Prescribe a coochie cream that you can't use on your coochie? That was five dollars and seventy-six cents thrown in the trash.

Moné: Well at least it's not *seventy-five* dollars and seventy-six cents thrown in the trash.

Vanity: Now you sho right about that! (They both laugh)

Voice Over: Gorilla screams

Vanity: You know that gorilla screaming *was* cute when we first got here but now it's starting to work my nerves. I thought with the ganja blending in with this vodka I'd be mellow by now but that gorilla is showing me (sing off key) it aaaint quiiite workin' juuust yeeet!

Moné: (chuckles) I'm just shocked you actually were willing to pay that much, out of pocket, for a prescription.

Vanity: Oh ta pft...You know I did ask if that was the generic brand. I just forgot to add that in the dialogue earlier. (They both laugh. Three seconds pass before vanity speaks)

Vanity: Isn't it funny? When you're fucking too much you get problems. When you're not fucking enough you get problems. I just can't seem to do right by my vajajay.

Voice Over: Gorilla screams

Moné: So, between being too wet and too dry, which do you prefer dealing with?

Vanity: Hmmm...Let's see. I guess it would depend on who I'm with.

Moné: Wait! Whaaaat? How does your malfunctioning genital have anything to do with who you're fucking?

Vanity: Glad you asked. Picture this (hands form a frame in the air) if he's too tiny (sticks up pinky finger) then being too moist is a problem 'cause he'll keep slippin' out. And if he's too large (hands form the letter C) being too dry when he's entering me would be worse than wiping my ass with sandpaper soaked in jalapeño pepper juice.

Voice Over: Gorilla screams

Moné: (Chuckling) So I guess celibacy is as foreign to you as "mathanese."

Vanity: Da fuck is mathanese?

Moné: Math written in Chinese...duuuh?

Vanity: Oh yeeeah...I remember what I was gonna tell you...I found out there's a Guinness world record for the man with the tiniest pecker?

Moné: How do you come up with this stuff?

Vanity: I am so not making this up. His name is Mike Carson. He's from Miami. He has a fully functioning penis at the size of 1/16 of an inch. (Pauses to think) Geesh...my clitoris is bigger than that though. Can you imagine? Him shooting sperm? That gotta be like the size of a tear drop. (Pauses to think again) Maybe I should seek him out. Wouldn't have to worry about gettin pregnant. Buuuuut...(looking off in wonder) getting with him would make me feel kinda gay...I imagine. (folding arms)

Moné: Da hell? (Looking baffled) What are you? A *cock* connoisseur?

Vanity: (hump shoulders, shakes head) I'm just sayin'.

Voice Over: Gorilla screams (Strange man walks up eating a sandwich. Biting down hard and pulling it from his mouth as if eating raw meat. He squeezes between Vanity and Moné. They give him the eye.)

Stranger: Yall gotta quarter? (Bite sandwich, chewing profusely)

Moné: Nope

Vanity: Naw

Stranger: Aaaaw come on now. (Bite sandwich, chewing erratically, swallow) Yall sittin outside this expensive ass restaurant, (bite, chew, swallow) drinking expensive ass drinks, (bite, chew, swallow) about to go inside and order expensive ass meals, (bite, chew, swallow) and seeing that yall glasses are almost empty yall most likely gonna order more expensive ass drinks (bite, chew, swallow) and from the looks of yas neither of yall intending on skippin those expensive ass desserts (bite, chew, swallow) from this expensive ass place (bite, chew, swallow) and yall aint got no quarter? (bite, chew, swallow)

Moné and Vanity: (Looks at the stranger with an irritated expression, rolling her eyes, but remains silent)

Stranger: This don't make no damn sense! (Puts last piece of sandwich in mouth, chews erratically, swallows, licks fingers and picks teeth.) I just can't believe this. Yall some broke ass motherfuckers! (wipes hands on pants, stands up, balls up the paper, tosses it in the air and kicks it before it hits the ground) Can't even give me a funky ass quarter!

Voice Over: Gorilla screams

Voice Over host: (Yells out) Moné and Vanity. (The ladies stand up to walk inside the restaurant)

Stranger: Well, ladies...can I at least *eat* yall...Oops! I mean eat *with* yall? (He laughs diabolically and goes to the next person to bug)

Vanity: Guuurrrl...I almost took him up on that offer. You saw how he ate the hell outta that sandwich. (Both bust up laughing)

Voice Over: Gorilla screams

END SCENE

NON-GOLDEN SILENCE

Did I say I love you in my last conversation with you?
Why does that matter now?
Ain't nothing either of us can do.
The nurse said she's taking her last breath.
Say what you need to cause she can still hear you.
How does she know that?
But you can't respond to prove it so does what I have to say really matter?
Are my verses putting you in better?
Isn't it only your words now that can truly matter?
Are my words going with you?
Because if you could speak now your words continue dwelling with me.
But you can no longer speak.
Or at least I can't hear you.
I'll just have to remember the last words you said.
That Obama is the president.
Your words were meaningless.
It's actually the sound of your voice that really matters now.
I still dream of you and you continue saying nothing.
All I want is to hear your voice...your spurts of unpredictable laughter.
Silence really isn't golden.

MISLAID MAMA

"Yes. Resuscitate her." My cousin replies, rudely interrupting my mental conversation. Though I disagree I remain silent.

After three days Mama came out of the comma. She had several bad seizures throughout the first night and now she says she's extremely sore. The nurse says Mama's muscles deteriorated so she'll need to be in a rehabilitative nursing facility for several months.

I sit at her bedside, looking up at the television. The nurse distributes Mama's medicines. She takes them without a fight today. I lift the plastic top that's covering her plate, to see what's for dinner. It's chili and a side of salad. I fix a towel under Mama's neck. She takes a spoon full of chili and swallows it. I ask her if she wants crackers. She softly says yes. I let her bite the corner of the saltine and wait until it looks like she's done chewing. I place another spoonful of chili into her mouth. I look up at the TV to see what the anchor man is reporting on the news. I'm just so disgusted with so much bad news. Different faces. Same tragedies.

I notice Mama has stopped chewing. A tear runs down her cheek. She appears to want to say something, but her mouth isn't opening.

"Ma! Are you choking?" I ask.

Mucus rattles in her throat. I see saliva trickling through the side of her lips but she's still not opening her mouth. I gently part her lips to see what is happening but her teeth are clenched. I try prying them apart. Nothing happens.

I roll myself quickly to the door and scream out, "HELP! NURSE!"

Two nurses run into the room. I explain that Mama appears to be choking. More tears trickle down Mama's cheeks, rendering me even more helpless.

As the one nurse is checking Mama's blood pressure and pulse, the other nurse asks, "Are you able to swallow?"

Mama nods her head.

She then asks, "Is there still food inside your mouth?"

Mama nods again.

"Are you trying to open up?" Another nod.

"Are you in any pain?" She shakes her head, no.

I let out a sigh of relief.

The nurse then announces, "It appears you have locked jaw."

I yell out, "Locked jaw! What caused that?"

The nurse responds, "Certain meds causes it. I'm pretty sure it was the Seroquel since that is one of the side effects."

The wind gets knocked out of me. I reply, "But...she's been taking Seroquel for years. Why the reaction now?"

An announcement comes into the room, through the wall speaker, stating the doctor is on the line to speak with the nurse. She excuses herself, and quickly walks out. I look at Mama, my heart continues shattering as I watch her suffer. "Mama I am so sorry this is happening to you."

The nurse returns to answer my question. "Apparently, when your mom took that overdose of Seroquel and went into a coma, the drug now has an adverse effect on her system. That was the doctor on the line. I explained to him what's happened. He says that she will no longer be given Seroquel."

I'm glad to hear this but I'm also concerned because Seroquel helps Mama sleep at night. If she doesn't sleep, she'll go into more psychotic episodes.

Thankfully, after a few more minutes of waiting, Mama's jaws open again, but of course she no longer wants to eat.

As if she hasn't gone through enough now the doctor says the diabetic sore on Mama's left ankle has gotten infected. They want to irrigate the area to clear the infection, in hopes of avoiding amputating her foot. The doctor says it'll be a quick procedure.

Some years ago, she broke her ankle falling down a flight of stairs. The bone went clear through her skin. She managed to suspend that leg in the air as her foot dangled. As she gripped the rails to hold her body up, I quickly grabbed the phone receiver from the wall and dialed 9-1-1. I then snatched a towel from the linen closet shelf and placed it under her foot. This allowed her to sit on the step as I gently laid her foot down. There was so much blood, but Mama sat there without shedding a tear. When the paramedics arrived, she asked, "It's pretty bad, huh?" It was so bad they had to operate twice to mend it properly.

On the day of her irrigation surgery my brother and sister arrive a short time after Mama was taken into the operating room. The medical staff says the procedure will only take an hour or so but it's been two and a half hours and no one has come out to give us the status. Nor is the waiting room monitor showing anything under Mama's assigned number.

Finally, a surgical staff lady comes out. She's asking dumb questions, like what is your mom's name, her date of birth, what surgical procedure was she getting? I'm thinking: WHAT THE FUCK... Shouldn't you already know all this shit! I talk myself into remaining calm because just like disgruntled chefs and waiters can spit, piss and shit in your food or drink out of retaliation I figure worse could happen to a loved one with these people if they become disgruntled. If Mama isn't dead, they'll probably kill her because of me, and I don't want to be my Mama's cause of death. Instead I say, "Lady, why are you asking me questions that you should already know?" She promises to bring in someone else who is better qualified to help us.

A second professional fuck up walks in exclaiming, "I'm truly sorry for the confusion. I know having your mom go through any type of surgery is nerve wrecking enough and now to have to go through this type of mix up..."

My sister blurts out. "There's no fucking mix up. You sons of bitches are starting to make me feel like you're stalling because you're covering some shit up. WHAT THE FUCK IS GOING ON WITH MY MOTHER?"

I'm thinking, oh, shit she may have just killed Mama and don't even know it. The second professional speaks again. "Okay I know you're upset but you really need to calm down. I can't help you if you don't cooperate with me. I have other things I could be doing but I chose to come in here."

My sister gets in his face. "I don't give a flying fuck about what else you could be doing! You motherfuckers better tell me what's going on with my Mama!"

The second professional turns red. "Ma'am...that's what I'm trying to do but you're shouting at me and it's impossible to speak while you're yelling. Now your mom apparently has been moved from the operating room. We've also checked with the nurses in the recovery room. They said your mom isn't there either..."

I chime in. "Why didn't someone come and tell me that she was moved. She's probably been back in her room all this time and we've been here. Oh God! She probably woke up looking for me!" I fly out the door.

My sister, brother and I take the elevator back to my Mama's room. Her bed is not there. We go to the nurse's desk and ask if she's been moved to a different room. She pushes buttons on the computer and asks for the date of birth and the room number. I tell her. She says, "There is no patient in our system with that information."

I tilt my head and nastily ask, "Ex-cuuuse me?! You were her nurse earlier this week." She replies. "Oh yes I remember. Isn't she still on the surgical unit?"

I look around and notice my sister is on her cell. My brother is leaning against the wall rubbing his temples. I do all I can to hold back tears. Instead of crying I scream. "SOMEBODY BETTER TELL ME WHERE THE FUCK MY MOM IS! I cannot believe you incompetent, unprofessional motherfuckers..."

My sister comes over. "You mean to tell me they can't find her?!" I shake my head.

She starts talking again on her cell. "Y'all need to get over here... now! These motherfuckers done mislaid Mama somewhere and can't fucking find her! Bout done mixed up her information with another patient and got her on the wrong gotdamn floor."

It isn't long before many of our relatives are swarming the halls and sitting in the room Mama was in before surgery. The head nurse is claiming they're doing all they can to find out what's going on. They even push in a cart of snacks–fruit, juice and crackers.

One of my cousins blurt out. “Nobody don’t want that shit. What they think they can calm us down after fucking losing my auntie… Ha!”

Finally, a doctor and police officer walks into the room. The doctor introduces himself as the chief physician. He asks us to follow him into a waiting room.

My aunt speaks out. “Naw…now why you just can’t tell us what’s going on right here?”

The police officer speaks up. “Ma’am visiting hours are officially over.”

Everyone begins gathering their things when I blurt out. “I’m not going nowhere till they tell me where my Mama is!”

The doctor responds. “We have located your mother and would like to speak with you all privately.”

As we are heading toward a private waiting room the police officer speaks again. “Technically you all should’ve been off this floor an hour ago. It is in everyone’s best interest to go to the waiting room. It really isn’t fair to the other patients for you all to still be here.”

Another irate cousin speaks. “Did he just say, “fair.” Fuck these other patients. These motherfuckers done lost my aunt. How fair is that shit?”

The police officer responds without turning around. “Watch your language sir!”

When we get into the waiting room some people sit, others stand. The doctor stare at the papers he’s holding. They’re shaking. He then looks around and asks who are Mama’s children? The three of us raise our hands. The doctor continues speaking in our direction. “Okay…um…according to the information I have your mom went in to have a procedure for an infection…”

I blurt out. “We already know that. Where is she NOW!”

He looks at me stunned. “I’m getting to that. I want to explain, step by step, so you can understand what happened…During the procedure they found that the infection had spread to her knee. They amputated her leg. Several of us gasp. The doctor continues.

"Apparently, after her procedure she was taken to the recovery room. Unfortunately, there were some complications."

I gasp and grab my mouth.

The doctor looks around. "Your mom's blood pressure dropped. Our staff did all we could to bring it back up. They succeeded in getting her blood pressure back to normal. But unfortunately, not long afterward her heart stopped. They did all they could to revive her.

"Your mom did not make it.
Her body is now in the morgue."

RELEASE

Everyone must leave here

You are not responsible for it

Nor can you cause it to happen

Release yourself NOW of any notion of guilt

of those who have already gone

And the many more who will go before you

Regardless of what you did or did not do prior to them leaving

It was meant to be and happened exactly as it was supposed to.

YOU ARE FINALLY FREE

NOW MOVE ON!

MODERN DAY BARTERING

I walk my dog through the neighborhood again, as is every day after I get off work. I walk with crutches, so I stroll slowly. I especially admire the homes made of brick, with their nicely manicured lawns. There are several that I pretend are mine.

That dream dissipates as I approach my one and half bedroom, basement apartment. I honestly don't know how I'm going to afford my own home on a measly $10,000 a year salary. I mean I could barely afford to pay $300 a month on rent, plus food, gas, light, telephone and other things I need to survive. Not to mention the way out of hand credit card debts. Daily, I'm scrambling my brain on how to buy my own home.

I think back on a conversation I overheard discussed by Clyde and his friend. Clyde is my cousin's boyfriend, and the father of her two children. "What's the point of putting money into investments and have to wait half your life to get extra pennies on it? That's just senseless...when I can double my money in a few days...tax free." He chuckles mockingly but his friend continues arguing his point that the way *he* invests is at least *legal.*

But what made no sense to me is how Clyde drives around in these fancy cars and living in a two-bedroom apartment. There is no way I'd have that kind of money and waste it like that. My own home and one car are all I need.

I wait until Clyde is alone before I approach him with my own investment idea. "You know Clyde with my brains and yo' money we could make some things happen around here."

His forehead wrinkles as if I'm talking in codes. I know he's wondering where I'm heading with this. I continue. "Okay. Let me start here. You know how I've been speaking about buying a house and eventually investing in real estate...right?" He nods. So, I continue. "But seeing I don't have a dime saved up and you have lots of cash and I have the credit we can work together on a real estate deal."

He finally has something to say. "That sounds nice and all, but I roll in cash only. Aint no bank accounts in my name so I can't write out no pretty li' checks to act like I'm a legit working-class nigga... I'm only ghetto rich and shit." He then leans forward to look directly into my eyes. "And I aint too quick to let a mufucka handle my loot."

I hope he don't think he's scaring me. I lean toward him. "I know about yo' reputation so why da fuck would I even be comin' to you with some bullshit fo?"

He relaxes and sits back comfortably in his chair. "Cool. Now that we both have that understandin'...Watchu talkin' bout li' Mama?"

He must have gotten me a bit intense cause I just realized my heartbeat feels like it's tapping my ribs.

I get animated now using my hands to help me talk. "Okay so first I would like to invest in your sidewalk pharmacy. So, I can save up enough to by me a house...in a nice neighborhood, 'cause I can't be dwelling in niggaville too much mo' longer. It's time to bounce. I figured if I can give you so much you can double it for me."

He stares at the floor as if he's waiting for me to say more. Okay I've stopped talking long enough now. He should know I'm waiting on his ass to respond. Okay now I'm gettin irritated. This mufucka look like he fell asleep with his eyes open. Wait...did this nigga stop breathing?

A few more seconds pass when he finally says. "Okay,"

I jump and reply, "Okay what?"

Now he's irritated. "Whatchu mean what? Give me yo money to invest?"

Now my forehead wrinkles. "You aint even said how much?"

He raises his eyebrows. "How much you got?"

My voice goes up an octave. "Ah hell naw!" We aint playin that game?"

He bursts into a guttural chuckle and smiles. It's such a pretty smile. Those celebrity white teeth make his even, chocolate skin tone pop. He continues smiling and says, "Okay li' Mama I gotchu. Let's start out with twenty-five hunerd."

I roll my eyes toward the ceiling. “Well damn! I just gave you my sob story about my measly ass salary and rent and utilities. Guess I forgot to mention I do have to supplement my income with credit cards. So those are maxed out. And the only reason I'm still able to even discuss this idea with you is ‘cause somehow, I'm able to save a few pennies here and there. Luckily, I don't have to pay a water bill ‘cause I'd be dead from dehydration by now.”

He clasps he hands together, leans his elbows on his knees, looks down at the floor then looks back up at me. “So how does that make you feel?”

Didn't know if I should respond or if he was just being flippant.

He starts again. “Okay…So if you want a fuckin' psychiatrist you need to head up there on Madison and Central, where you can get all the head doctors, dentists and any other welfare white coat wearin' wannabe mufuckas you need. You came to me about business. I honestly don't give a fuck about yo lack. Either you in or you aint.”

I pucker my lips wonderin' how the hell am I gonna come up with that kinda money. I tell him. “I'm in.”

The next day I go to my good ol' secure ass, great benefits ass, everybody envy ass, boring as federal government ass job. I knew this place was gonna stifle me emotionally. On the first day I began as a clerk-typist. I got diarrhea and the toilet overflowed. Thankfully, I was able to get out of there without slipping in my own shit. And since no one else was in there no one ever found out it was me.

But my misery is the least of my worries right now. As long as I got this job, I can make myself happy in my own home. And since I was able to co-sign for three different people's cars–both of my siblings and my cousin's boyfriend–my plan is to finally do something for myself. The killing part about co-signing for everybody else's car is I am unable to drive neither one of them, or should I say my cars, because I need to use hand controls. Hand controls clasp on the brake and accelerator for people with disabilities who are unable to use their legs.

I approached one of my close co-worker friends, Shanola. We often hang out for lunch and after work. So, she knows my family and friends. I explained to her, “Clyde is going to hook me up by doubling my money on his investment, but I don't have enough money." We both have high aspirations, so it doesn't take long for her to decide that she wanted in. We both agree to come up with $1,250 each by next payday.

When payday comes, Shanola gives me fresh bills. I meet up with Clyde over the weekend and give him $2,500. Of course, I lecture *him* this time. "Just like you don't want to be fucked. Don't fuck me, Clyde."

His voice gets high pitched. "Girl what is you talkin' bout? You know I aint on no bullshit. You know what I'm sayin'. I aint on dat, li' Mama."

I nod my head in agreement. "Yeah. I already know you good people. That's why I felt comfortable comin' to ya."

About two weeks pass. I get a call from Clyde. I walk from my apartment to meet him at his apartment, which by the way, is also in my name. I did it for my cousin and her children's sake.

My cousin is there with her two baby boys who are barely a year apart. I play with them until Clyde hands me a wad of money, separated in rubber bands—mostly in $20 bills and still too many in $5 and $1 bills. I'm stunned. "What the hell..." I say.

He responds. "Whatchu thought you was gettin back...crisp clean bills like from yo checkin' account withdrawals?" He busts up laughing and continues. "You forgot I deal with crack heads so aint no telling what might be on this money." He chuckles.

My stomach turns just thinking of all the possibilities.

I count it all out. Some is wrinkled and ripped. Some is taped up. But it all adds up to $5,000 as he promised. I smile, hold out my hand, he shakes it and smiles. I tell him thank you.

And let him know I'll be doing more business with him soon. I stuff some in each side of my bra and some down my panties. I walk back to my apartment.

I take my co-worker her portion. She says she wants to reinvest. So, we do it all over again—several times. I pay off all my credit card debts and I'm able to give hefty monetary Christmas gifts to my family. Of course, they question me but I'm wise enough not to answer them.

I want to make enough for a nice deposit on a new home. I wanna cut my co-worker out so I tell her I'm going to double the amount hoping to discourage her. But that didn't work. Now I'm transporting $5,000 from the job back to my apartment.

As I'm heading toward the apartment to give Clyde the money. There's a police car parked at the corner. I've been told that if cops find a lot of money on you, they question you. If your answer doesn't suffice then they could assume what they want and lock you up. I know I don't have anything to worry about since I work for the feds, but still I don't want to have to deal with the drama. I've also heard that if you don't have any money on you the cops can lock you up for being a vagrant. So damned if you do and damned if you don't. Just another law created to screw Blacks over.

As I get closer to the corner, I can see a cop sitting in the car. He opens his door and steps out. I slow down to watch where he's going. He's heading toward Clyde's building. I ponder if I should turn around and go back home. I continue walking to Clyde's apartment. Thankfully the cop goes to the alley behind the building.

I hit their doorbell and they take forever buzzing me in. When I get inside, I ask them if they know why the cops are outside? They both say no. I tell them, "I started to turn around and go back home."

"Li' Mama whatchu worried about?"

I tell him I don't want them questioning me about nothin'. He assures me I have nothing to worry about. So, I let it go.

Weeks pass and he tells me he got my package. Instead of handing me the money he starts talking about the landlord has been questioning them as to why I'm never at the apartment? I ask them what did they say? My cousin said she told them I work a lot. I suggest that maybe I should start being there when he comes to pick up the rent. Clyde says he doesn't think that's necessary. I drop it but I'm still uncomfortable about it.

Clyde hands me a huge bundle and I'm flabbergasted. I get over the suspicious landlord quick. It's late and I'm sleepy. I tell Clyde, "I'll just count it when I get back home." So, I begin unwinding the rubber bands and stuffing sections of the money in various parts of my underwear.

Aw naw li' Mama. I don't want no problems. If you get home and it's not all there, you'll swear I screwed you. Gone count it out now. It aint gone take you that long."

I do it. It took longer than I wanted but all $10,000 of it is accounted for. I step outside and there is a cop car again. When I get home, I call my cousin to tell her about the cop's car. She giggles and tell me I need to stop being so paranoid.

I'm at my good "ol' govment" job again when I get a call on my work line. It's my cousin's landlord or my *other* landlord I should say. After feigning being cordial, he asks, "Are you actually living in the apartment?"

I don't know why I'm stunned. I don't want to lie but I don't want my cousin to be put out on the streets either. So, I repeat what my cousin said, "I'm rarely there because I have to work."

Apparently, this doesn't work. He continues. "But even when I go there on Saturdays you're not there still. You work six days a week?"

Now I want to cuss him out but instead I say, "I do work on Saturdays...sometimes." He then starts in. "Well, I've been asking around and some of the other tenants are saying you live around the corner and only come to visit your cousin a couple of hours in the evening.

Oh shit, people are snitching on me. I wonder what else they know. When I don't respond he continues. "You are aware you signed the lease stating you will be residing in the apartment. If you're not living there, you're breaching the agreement and I could have the lease terminated and take you to court."

I panic. "Take me to court for what?"

He gets loud. "Breaching the contract is against the law. I could have your cousin evicted and sue you for the remaining payments for the months due on the lease."

All I could say is, "I understand."

After we hang up, I call my cousin. I don't even say hello when she picks up. "Your landlord just called me asking if I live there."

She asks, "What did you tell him?"

I tell her and include my solution. "Maybe I should stay overnight when he comes to get the rent."

She snaps. "Girl it aint that serious. He just talkin' shit. As long as he gettin' that money da fuck he care who's paying it."

She's a bit too unconcerned for me. I may be miserable at this job but I'm not trying to fuck myself out of it until I could do better.

I snap. "Girl! He's talkin' about suing me. I'm not tryna mess myself up. I'm trying to get me a house and that could go on my credit."

She starts in. "There you go getting' all paranoid..."

I cut her off. "Okay I'll talk to you when I get off work." I slam the phone a little too hard.

I have another $5,000 for Clyde to double but I also want to discuss the landlord's call again. Apparently, my cousin just doesn't get how this situation could possibly jeopardize my life. When I get to the corner before their apartment there are cops sitting inside their car again. I continue to their apartment. As soon as I get inside, I hand Clyde the money. As he's counting it, I tell him about the cop car. He doesn't respond. I then mention the conversation I had with the landlord.

He stops counting the money, leans back in his seat and rubs his hands along his legs, before speaking. "You know li' Mama...look like this startin' to be a bit too much fa ya."

Not quite the response I was expecting. So, I seek clarification. "Whatchu mean?"

He takes some time to respond, as if choosing his words carefully. "I'm just sayin' you seem like you worried and all. You gettin' all worked up about the cop just sittin' outside. You feel like the landlord is really gonna do somethin' to ya."

Okay apparently, he ain't getting it either. I ask. So, it don't seem suspicious to you that every time I'm coming and leaving here the cops are out there? And now that the landlord's sayin' people are watching me you don't think that's something to be concerned with?"

He responds. "Naw...not at all. Aint nobody seein' nothin'. Plus, they can't prove it."

I say, "Well I'm startin' to get uncomfortable about all this."

He picks the money up to begin counting it again and continues talking. “Well li’ Mama we should just chill from doin’ this again. So, we’ll make this the last time.”

Not quite what I wanted to hear. My goal was to stop when I had $20,000. Well at least I got all my credit cards paid off. The rest of the cash will stay safe in my safe deposit box at the bank until I’m ready to buy my house. I’ll be letting the government deduct additional money from my paycheck for savings bonds. Wouldn’t want them asking me questions about having a large sum of cash deposited all at once into my checking account.

ASSIS-TIVE LET-TER-ING

I can appreciate the num-ber-ing and ti-tling
Which were/are words assis-ting in crea-ting
Major tormen-ting for you
It is a unique shif-ting of sent-en-cing
In third person you are wri-ting
Then swit-ching back to first person
Mak-ing the mon-o-loguing quite mind blow-ing
Quo-ting extremely upset-ting dia-loguing
Resem-bling machete body pier-cing
Horrendous layers of skin-ning

Your own voice in your head repea-ting
And/or merely mirro-ring someone else's opinon-ing
Beautifully expres-sing your fee-lings
Part one abruptly interrup-ting the torment-ting
Asking mom for a straighten-ing device
Creat-ing your best solution of cea-sing endless hur-ting
Part two the boyfriend reinfor-cing jealousy
Bring-ing out the ass-holing due to chea-ting
Body sha-ming additional ago-ni-zing
Supplementary brain tor-turing

Insecurities increase simply due to compar-ing
Fal-ling prey via li-ving through social media ly-ing
Asteris-king "double tap" evokes great imagi-ning
Erec-ting frustra-ting events which is non-exis-ting
Everyone rela-ting to degra-ding, preten-ding and compe-ting
Especially when belie-ving unrealities
It would be interes-ting in rea-ding
You dig-ging deeply in tel-ling via wri-ting
Others experien-cing various ha-ting
In *your* exact same format-ting!

MASSAGE GINNY

It seems that everyone is having issues with their spouses. Geesh...is no one happily married these days? I mean one client complains their spouse isn't adventurous enough in the bedroom. Another client swears their spouse is cheating because no one works that much and remains that energetic after returning home, near midnight, seven days a week. Well I guess I shouldn't complain, because if they were all happy and loving at home, I wouldn't have an influx of clients.

I used to love my job. Meeting and talking with new people, helping them ease their tensions. But then some started scaring me with talks of outrageous violence. I tried allowing them to get comfortable by calling me by my first name, Ginny. But they became too comfortable with our conversations and acted as if I was *their* girlfriend or something. So, I attempted maintaining a level of respect by having them call me Ms. Ginny. That still didn't work. Apparently, many of my male clients only see Women as property. No matter how the conversation starts out it always takes a demeaning twist.

For instance, for confidentiality, I'll call this client, Jack. Jack is talking so fondly of his wife—how she adores him. She makes sure his dinner is ready for him when he gets home from work, every evening. And how she even makes his bath water just like he likes it. But then he goes on to say if more men *trained* their Women properly, there would be fewer divorces. I want so badly to say, "Yeah, you're such an expert but you're here with me...every week."

As Jack continues talking, I spot activity outside my window. I say excuse me in hopes that jack would stop talking for possibly three seconds. But he doesn't. I pull the curtain back to peek out. I can see it's Jonathan heading back across the street. I've been with him for over five years now. His level of jealousy and distrust is becoming unbearable. I made the mistake of telling him details about my duties with the clients. I mean he's the one who talked me into getting into this type of work in the first place.

I go back to sit down. Under respectable circumstances I would've apologized and asked, "Where were we?" But since Jack never shuts up, I'm convinced he didn't even notice me walk away. But now I've totally zoned out and have lost focus. Jonathan's presence throws me off from concentrating on anything...every time. I know there's going to be problems when I get home.

I notice a quick few seconds of quiet. Jack has finally shut up. I jump in, "You know we've gone fifteen minutes past the hour, but I won't charge you extra...this time."

He thanks me, gets dressed, and flirtatiously tells me, "Charge our *session* to my account." He chuckles.

I giggle back and say, "As always." I fail to mention I've added additional bullshit fees in the process, which I hope he never notices. I see him out, and lock the door.

I look back out the window. I watch Jack get into his car. I look around, checking to see if Jonathan may still be lurking. Thankfully he's not.

My clients who are doctors, or work in executive positions, or partners in law firms oftentimes use their corporation's credit card for my personal services. So, I have to mask my business activities as "Stress Management Seminars" or "Office Supplies" or "Procedural Addendum Brochures."

Likewise, my married clients prefer using the cover name, "Sports and Fitness" to avoid the wrath of their wives. What my services boil down to is massages, discussions, and a few glasses of my client's favorite wine, which helps relieves stress.

I straighten up the office, pack my things and shut off the lights before leaving. I dread having to face Jonathan, so I drive below the posted speed limit all the way home. The vehicles behind me are blowing their horns. Once they realize I'm not changing my pace for them they quickly drive around. Some drive next to me to take time to throw up their middle finger and mouth obscenities. I then turn on my hazard lights, in hopes of avoiding the rigmarole. What usually takes me fifteen minutes to get home, turns into 30 minutes. Still not long enough.

I walk into the house and smell spaghetti sauce brewing. Fuck! Jonathan's already here. I head to the master bathroom, hoping he's still in the kitchen cooking. I shower and put on fresh lingerie as he requires me to do as soon as I get in.

I grab the doorknob to step out the bathroom and Jonathan is standing in the doorway. Eyes wide, and nostrils flaring as he takes deep breaths. He says, "Hey babe. Glad you made it home safely."

I freeze. Not knowing what he really means because nothing is ever clear with him. Just when I think I got him all figured out he flips on me.

"*That-was-a-compliment*." He stresses each word.

My voice shakily responds, "Thank you." But he pretends he didn't hear me.

"What was that MYSOGYNY? Oh...I'm so sorry. I mispronounced your business name again. Didn't I, *Massage Ginny*?"

I repeat thank you a bit louder.

His body relaxes as he says, "Great! Dinner is almost done. I started it for you. You can finish it. I'm hungry. Do you know how much longer it'll be?"

I look at him puzzled. I don't even know what he's cooking. How in the hell am I supposed to know how much longer? I respond, "Not long."

I follow him to the kitchen. The table is set so nicely. Candles are burning. Soft classical jazz music plays on the Alexa echo speaker. Some pots are on the stove with the fire set to low.

My goal is to make sure I do and say any and everything to keep him happy. So, I speak with insincere enthusiasm, "This set up is beautiful. Thank you. So, what are we having?"

He replies, "Go check it out."

Just as I head toward the stove, he grabs me around the waist, holding me from behind. He whispers in my ear. "You must be some kind of special bitch to make me go all out my way like this."

I repeat thank you, but sensuously this time.

He lets me go and I continue walking toward the stove. I see it is spaghetti and meatballs. I drain the water from the spaghetti. Transfer the sautéing meatballs into the simmering tomato sauce and stir it. I then fix a big bowl of tossed salad.

When everything is done, Jonathan pulls my chair out. He says grace and we eat. He pours us both a half glass of sangria.

He sips, then asks, “So how much did you make today?”

I cringe and respond. “I haven't had time to check it yet.”

He puts his glass down. “And why is that?”

I gently put my fork down to explain. “Look Jonathan can we just finish dinner before...”

He interrupts. “Oh, so what you're saying is I'm bothering our dinner by asking you this simple question?”

I put a fork full of spaghetti and a piece of meatball into my mouth but have difficulty swallowing.

He continues getting louder. “You know you're always making things so much more harder than they have to be. You enjoy making a big scene out of everything. I mean...counting money before coming home shouldn't be an ordeal...ev-er-y fu-cking day...really! Your clients come in. You do your thing. You get the cash. *They* go. Then repeat. As soon as the last one leaves. You count the cash. You lock up. Then *you* go! Okay well just give me a rough estimate of about how much you think you made today?”

This time I drop the fork on the plate and gently rub my fingers along the side of my forehead before responding. “It's really hard to say Jonathan, because some clients include tips.”

Jonathan slams his glass down. Surprisingly it doesn't break. “So, let me get this straight...” He places his hands together, so that the fingertips are touching. “It sounds to me like you're saying...a client hands you money...and you don't even bother to count it, to be sure they paid you properly.”

“I always count the cash. It's the debit and credit card transactions I'm not sure of. Sometimes they include the tip on the receipt, after they sign it, and I haven't checked the receipts yet.”

He jumps to his feet. “GODDAMNIT GINNY.” He dives over the table. I attempt to quickly stand up to get out of his way. Too late.

He slams me to the floor, while I'm still in the sitting position in my chair. He's strangling me. Vomit spews from my mouth. He slams my jaw into the floor. Desperately trying to free my face from the floor he smashes my lips into my vomit. The more I squirm, the more my head slides, the harder he smashes my face.

He snatches my head up by my hair. From my side view I could see his pants are around his ankles. He slaps my face with his erect penis. "Now suck it!" He demands.

I slowly reach for it. He shoves it down my throat. I pull my head back. "Did I tell you to stop!" He slaps my face. Yellow chunks spew from my throat again.

He drags me by my hair into the bedroom. I try standing to ease the excruciating pain searing through my scalp. "Bitch! You will continue to crawl as long as you're in my presence!" He yanks and twists my head, forcing me to scurry on my hands and knees. I feel a pop, hoping a bone in my spine only cracked and didn't break.

He throws me across the bed, I land on my back. He snatches my arms so that my head is hanging over the edge of the bed. He straddles over me, rams his now limp penis down my throat.

Choking, I flip my legs up and over, so that my body lands alongside of him. I end up on the floor, vomiting more. This time it's liquids.

He's more pissed now. "Ooooh....So, now you're a gymnast...huh hoe! Well let me help you with that!"

He grabs my legs. Turning me upside down, tackling me like a football player, he rams my body into the wall. "Now put it back in your throat!" He screams.

After what felt like an hour of this torture, he finally walks out the house, slamming the door, as if he were the one being tortured.

I sit on the floor, gazing at the wall where he slammed my body. Parts of the drywall is indented; white flakes are crumbled on the carpet. Him ramming me into the wall was a slight relief. I mean, it meant one less punch I had to take to my face. Although I don't have a bloody and broken nose this time, doesn't mean my eye socket isn't damaged. There's an on and off burning sensation in my left eye now. It feels like my tonsils are bleeding. I try to place a finger on the sore spot and gag. I think the skin is broken. My side hurts so bad I think another one of my organs is hemorrhaging.

I'm afraid one day he'll succeed in killing me. He broke my jaw once. Then another time he pulled a patch of hair from my scalp. It hasn't grown back since. He's even pissed on me a few mornings, announcing, "This is your new alarm clock." He spat mucous into my coffee, and forced me to drink it. But the worst was when he smeared his diarrhea into my eyes, nose and mouth, because he shit his pants one morning, when he couldn't make it to the bathroom in time. The wrath of his evilness is endless. What's worse is I never know when he's going to strike again.

I was only able to share this with a few people. But that was a useless waste of breath because what could they do? Everyone is just as scared as I am of him. It looks even worse for

me to discuss his violent treatment of me and I'm the sole bread winner. I guess I must look awfully damn stupid being the one making the money and not being able to use it because he takes it.

I've decided, this is it. I gotta get away. I cannot continue going through this. This will be about my seventh attempt at leaving. Trying to get out of this abusive marriage is going to be like trying to get out of a burning home, while all the doors and windows are consumed by fire. I'm subject to die if I stay here.

According to the National Domestic Violence Hotline statistics show that 1 in 4 women (24.3%) and 1 in 7 men (13.8%) aged 18 and older in the United States have been victims of severe physical violence by an intimate partner in their lifetime. Females ages 18 to 24 and 25 to 34 generally experienced the highest rate of intimate partner violence... About 4 in 5 victims of intimate partner violence were female. Most female victims of intimate partner violence were previously victimized by the same offender.

If you or someone you know are victims of domestic violence and would like to get help there is 24-hour help nationwide.

-

National Domestic Violence Hotline

http://www.thehotline.org
Voice: (800) 799-7233
TTY: (800) 787-3224
Illinois relay service for the deaf and hearing-impaired dial 711
All other states dial
(800) 526-0844 for relay services
Video Phone: (855) 812-1001

Date: Februever 4, 8888

TO: All Manipulators/Exploiters/Spiritual Vampires/Evil Doers/ Egotistical Azzholes

FROM: Selfless Givers, Empaths and Sincere at Heart

SUBJECT: DUMBASS OF DECEPTION

This is a reminder to all who seek to swindle and harm people who are selfless givers, empaths and sincere at heart. Trust and believe that a loving and kind hearted person is far from stupid. They can smell bullshyt oozing from your pores and eking from your breath as you continuously say things in hopes of luring them into your phukery.

Your goal is to get them to do things that would benefit ONLY you while sabotaging them. They can clearly see that your words do not match your actions. What you fail to realize is that although they are listening, they are also laughing inside because they already know it is just a matter of time before your shyt hits the floor and you are the ONLY one stepping in it. The best part is you'll be the ONLY one cleaning it up. The second-best part is the loving hearted get to watch you clean up your own shyt, that you created, which was intended for them.

Oh, ye dumbass of deception you cannot keep doing wrong and expecting to get right results! When will you finally learn that karma is still real? If not now...soon...very soon! And if it does not get you directly it will hit you indirectly through a loved one or something you love excessively–like your ego.

I am confident that you will be forever ungrateful for this reminder.

You're Welcome Anyway

I AM ENOUGH

Of
ALL
of
the
trillions
of
living
organisms
that
exist
I
Was
Formed.
It
is
miracles
such
as
being
born
which
is
all
that
is
required
to
prove
that

I am enough!

(Read that again until you finally believe it)

STACKED CELL HOLES

We are lounging in my brother's bedroom. I gotta pee so I climb down from the bed and scoot towards the bathroom when someone yells out, "Sumbody comin!" We scramble to get back into position. My brother and two of our friends are ducked under the windowsill.

I go back to stand on the bed to get tensely tucked behind an opened tattered curtain. A petite framed lady wearing a mini skirt, the length of daisy duke shorts1 is approaching. She severely tosses her hips as she struts. The man walking beside her, steps with an exaggerated dip, looking as if he could fall over.

They are less than a half block away. The lady's afro seems to grow the closer she gets. A perfectly rounded, cushiony egg nest. I'm hoping it lands right in the center. My brother's friend lifts his body just enough to stick his arm through the erratically circular, skull sized hole in the window screen. His face scrunches as he throws the egg with as much force as he could muster.

SPLAT! We each peek to check the results. It lands right at the heel of her pencil thin, stiletto sandal. We quickly duck, and tuck again. A few seconds go by and I inch back out to see what the lady is doing. She points her finger, counting the floors up.

As if she spotted us the ranting begins. "You li' nappy headed ass bastards need to be savin' those eggs fo' yo' fat funky ass mammy!"

We're all snickering. Now I really gotta pee. I whisper, "Oh no...I think she saw me." My brother shushes me as if she could hear us all the way from the fifth floor.

Of all of the other egged victim attempts, she lingers the longest. I think I've broken a world record, this time, for holding my pee so long. She continues letting us have it, despite the man's pleading and tugging her arm in an attempt to get her to resume walking. I could swear she's creating new cuss words.

When she's finally out of sight we burst out screaming with laughter. We waited hours to get this response–a phenomenal cussing out. I can finally go pee. I scoot to the bathroom.

In 1972, I was four years old, my brother was ten and my sister was nine. Ma moved us into the Rockwell Gardens public housing projects at 2501 West Monroe, apartment 513.

Built in 1958, the name "Gardens" was due to the vast award-winning flowerbeds that residents thoroughly enjoyed. This community, named East Garfield Park, consisted of eight buildings, ranging from ten to thirteen stories high, with 1,126 apartments.

Due to the Great Depression and World War II, homes deteriorated. In 1949, Congress passed the Housing Act. In 1950, residents were displaced so that the Congress (Eisenhower) Expressway could be constructed. The goal was for the Chicago Housing Authority (CHA) to provide several thousand units of temporary housing for veterans but a white aldermen refused plans for public housing in their wards. As a result, CHA built family housing in Black residential areas only.

The racial segregation embodied in these developments complied with federal policy (the Neighborhood Composition Rule), which required that the tenants of a housing development be of the same race as the people of the area in which it was located.

At first managers were selective in choosing among the thousands of families who applied for apartments. As time passed managers lost interest in being selective. This is when things take a turn for the worse.

CHA's main concern was that there was one employed breadwinner and that the tenants behave according to prescribed rules. Ma was not an employed breadwinner, but she was an

ADC (Aid to Dependent Children) recipient who was a stickler for rules. Continuously instilling her moral beliefs onto us. "Say the Lord's prayer before going to bed...Don't leave the house wearing dirty or holey underwear...Treat people how you want to be treated." She even remained consistent when preparing the same meals on certain days of the week, and completing required chores, such as going to the laundromat every Thursday and grocery shopping every Saturday.

I'll never forget once when she went to the corner grocer and returned home only to find that the cashier gave her too much change back. Ma walked right back to the store to return the money. This seemed like the craziest thing ever to me especially since she's always saying she didn't have money to do extra stuff.

When I was about six years old, Ma was going either to the currency exchange, the grocery store or both, but my brother didn't go with her this particular time. She returned home staggering. She remembered a man grabbing her brown paper bag, in which she carried cash and food stamps, instead of a purse, hoping to fool muggers. She said she screamed, while holding tightly to the bag. He got scared, let go of the bag and ran off. When she woke up, she was sitting at the bottom of the concrete steps. There was blood on her collar because the back of her head was bleeding. She refused to go to the hospital despite her hurting hip and the possibility of having a concussion. Because she awakened on the step, we believe she hit her head on the metal handrail.

Although the robber did not succeed with taking what little we had, he succeeded in taking Ma's ability to walk straight because she was in so much pain. He also took our privilege of having the luxury of hot meals. We ate sandwiches for weeks until Ma got better. That attempted robbery could've taken more from us than food stamps and money had Ma died on those steps. **An incident like this makes even a child appreciative, regardless of having less, as long as the healthy lives of loved ones are still present.**

But Ma's spirit remained high and she managed to keep us entertained within the comforts of our jail cell type apartment. We played cards, board games, hand clapping and slapping games and when we got bored with these, and she went to bed, we made up our own games–usually inspired by TV.

But not today because there is a breaking news report on every channel! Walter Cronkite is talking about how President Nixon's leadership has failed. He is going to tell the nation that he is quitting because of something called a stupid Watergate scandal. Ugh! No one cares about this shit! We can't even watch any of our usual programs–"Good Times," "All in the Family," "The Jeffersons."

This news crap is talking about people broke into the White House. I don't see what the big deal is. No one was hurt like Ma was when she almost got robbed. And no one was killed like some of my neighbors were during robberies.

Listening to the news makes me wonder are the criminals in my community mimicking the criminals in the White House or vice versa? I catch words from the news reporter like plumbing, bugging and deep throat and something about papers being stolen. At first, I wondered what any of this got to do with us? But now I can relate to the stolen papers part because someone almost stole Ma's food stamp booklet too.

Our friends are over early, which is typical since their mom is hardly home. Ma usually makes our food stretch so that they can eat too. We watch TV but the one commercial that keeps playing most, between episodes of the Saturday morning cartoons, is the "Wam-O-Slip-N-Slide" commercial. Every time the Slip-N-Slide commercial airs our determination to escape into that life escalates. The announcer's voice is monotonous yet choppy as he emphasizes certain words to aid in our excitement:

> The Wam-O-Slip-N-Slide. It's unbelievable and it's for you. It's new. It's magic. Just unroll the Wam-O-Slip-N-Slide. Hook up to any water faucet and the magic surface goes to work. It's fast. It's easy. You glide on a thin film of water and it makes you go like a jet. **Girls glide as well as boys**. Thin roll it's cool summer splashing fun. Get yours today. The famous Slip-N-Slide by Wam-O.

We imagine out loud, claiming the direction we'd turn while sliding across that water splattered plastic. My brother says, "All we need is a long piece of plastic."

His friend chimes in. "We don't need no water hose just throw down water."

I tell them, "Ma put the shower curtains on the shelf." We don't have a shower, just a bathtub, so there was never a need for curtains.

As soon as Ma goes to bed my brother grabs the two plastic curtains, spreads them across the tile covered concrete floor, pours water down, and voila our homemade, indoor Slip-N-Slide is born. We all strip down to our underwear. My brother runs and dives. But is disappointed to come to a screeching halt in mid slide. We all burst out laughing.

His friend tries but fails. They pour down more water and try again. Same result. My brother determines that the underwear is preventing a smooth slide, so he strips naked.

The rest of us protest with disgust but once we see that he slides further and with ease, we figure naked is the solution. Sitting down, I forcefully push myself, with my hands, across the wet plastic. I glide uncontrollably almost slamming against the couch. I didn't break anything, so I go at it repeatedly.

The next day we all have foreign pieces of debris in our butt cheeks. But it was so worth it!

In the projects we all shared similar joyous moments, miserable experiences and even face or actually experience potential horrible fates. It's sad we weren't more compassionate towards one another in an attempt to make life a bit more pleasant. Instead, loved ones seem to have become even more brutal toward one another.

I'm only ten years old now. All I want is to enjoy doing fun things—not grow up so fast. It's like other peoples' pain becomes my actual experiences.

Several nights I had to listen to Patricia whimper as Harry uses her as a punching bag. Although they are standing on the porch their voices sound as if they're inside our living room. Between soft whimpering and deep breaths, she keeps repeating, "Okay...I'm sorry Harry." Perhaps her apologies are pissing him off even more because he's yelling, "Patricia, didn't I tell you befo' bout dat bullshit, huh?" Smacking her again.

When their voices fade, and we think *he*'s finally had enough her sobs start again. My sister turns out the lights to peek behind the shade to see where they are. She's careful not to rattle the metal bars so they won't hear her.

Patricia is our neighbor who lives in the corner cell next to ours. I don't understand why her mother can't hear her. She should've come out already.

I ask my brother, "Why won't you go and help her."

He replies, "I'm not gettin in dat."

I ask Ma, "Can we call the police to stop him."

She replies, "That aint our business. Donchu know people will kill you for meddlin in their business?"

Now I'm frustrated. "But Ma what if that was one of us? Wouldn't you want someone to help us?"

She replies, "Let's just pray that never happens to yall. Like I tolchu befo' if somebody hits you and you can't whoop 'em pick up somethin' and try to knock the shit out of 'em."

Apparently, like Ma, another resident was conflicted with the fear of minding somebody else's business:

> ...When you in the projects, you do a lot of things, you see a lot of things, but you know you don't wanna say nothing because it can get you hurt...but it be on your conscience, and it drives me crazy when I can't say nothing...I see this little boy, he's about 12 years old. He's shooting, I see him shooting at the others (kids). And I'm looking at this, and I know his mother and everything. Everybody telling me, "No, don't say nothing, don't tell his mother." And now he's dead, the little boy is dead now, and it made me feel if I had a told his mother, maybe he'd still be here.

Minding your own business comes easy for many but the frustration, fear and regret of not getting involved comes with emotional costs. The fact that we have now become that fearful, non-helpful neighbor bothers me profoundly.

My brother continuously watches re-runs of Elvis Presley's movies. He purchased a tape recorder to record the sound tracks from various movies. His favorite movie and song are "Jailhouse Rock." He jerks his head, twirls and wriggles his legs, torso and arms, points his fingers and toes in a pathetic attempt to mimic Elvis. I burst up laughing at him but silently compliment him because he actually moves pretty good.

Elvis plays the character of Vincent Everett portraying a tough guy who fights his way to fame and fortune. The musical jailhouse scene makes prison sound and look like a fun place. The prop is a two-story replica of jail cells. A facsimile of where I live.

I remember overhearing adults say that Rockwell Gardens was modeled after prison. The huge rectangular bricks are also used in public facilities such as courts, schools, and hospitals. The floors and ceilings are supported with concrete and metal. The metal door is the only door to enter and exit the cell. Although the bedrooms have wooden doors, there were no doors on the closets. Nor was there a door on the oversized brick, shelved, cubby hole used as a pantry in the kitchen and makeshift linen closet.

The porches had tall chain linked fences, which was possibly meant for our safety. However, that one fence was not enough because there is a second wrought iron fence, with tiny holes, overlapping the chain linked fence. This was erected to stop people from throwing things over or perhaps from throwing themselves over.

Mr. Winters, a former tenant, refers to the apartments as "hell holes stacked on top of each other." The only thing missing from these jail cell type apartments are the guards. As a result, crime escalated:

gang activities
drug dealings
prostitution
muggings
rape
murder
suicide, etc.

Since the Violence Against Women Act (VAWA) does not pass until 1994 Domestic Violence cannot be listed as part of the escalated criminal activities in Rockwell Gardens.

We got a new cool neighbor, who is a mother about Ma's age. She let us drink and smoke cigarettes at her house. Another neighbor, who was only a year older than me, showed me how to smoke marijuana and we drank together. Sometimes we'd sneak a can of Ma's beer and her cigarettes to drink and smoke in my brother's bedroom.

Once we were tipsy enough and bored, and Ma finally goes to sleep, the fun continues. We'd play with the rotary telephone. My brother learned how to do Morse codes after watching some TV show, I believe it was M*A*S*H, so he shows me and our friends. We were actually able to call people by swiftly counting out and depressing the hang up button, pausing, then swiftly pressing repeatedly until it rings.

Not having any luck finding fun people to talk to we grabbed the oversized telephone book. Closing our eyes, we'd point to a number. By the way the telephone book is versatile as it is also used to boost babies sitting at the dinner table.

My brother goes first. He says in a deep southern drawl, "Cook County morgue. You kill 'em, we fill 'em." As if they called him. We all hear the CLICK and bust up laughing.

It's my turn. I don't tell them, but I actually call a school friend's number. Her mother cusses us out way worse than the egged victim. We roar with laughter and keep calling her back until my brother makes us stop.

I then call a number from the phone book. The man on the other end, speaking with a deep guttural bear like voice, asks me, "What are you wearing sweetheart?"

Disgusted, I look at the receiver. My brother asks, "What he say?" I tell him.

My brother's friend snatches the phone and yells, "You sick pervert! You're the one who be ova der suckin' on Ms. Rivers legs." Ms. Rivers is one of our old, wrinkled neighbors who we're always poking fun about. My brother shushes his friend so he wouldn't wake Ma. His friend slams the phone down on the cradle and we all bust up laughing.

When I turn thirteen years old, I rarely get to enjoy doing teen things, like wasting hours playing video games, attending parties, and talking on telephone party lines, where potential boyfriends are found. This is because we can't afford video games. Ma won't let me go anywhere that could lead to danger. A few times I did call the party line and stayed on too long. She got extremely angry with me for running the phone bill up ridiculously high. But she was able to call the telephone company to explain the situation. They removed the charges and blocked our phone from being able to call the party line again.

I decided to take a break from reading in my bedroom all day. So, I opt to sit on the porch. It is a beautiful summer day. I stare out into the former playground where people are mingling. I say former because where the swings used to be there are several dangling chains holding a leather black strap where a seat once was. The merry go round aint so merry no more as one side has been kissing the ground for years. Though the slide is dented it's still slidable, but the steps have disappeared. So, the only way up the slide is to step up the way you're supposed to only slide down. At least there is still a bench to sit on. The paint that was once striped rainbow colors of yellow, red and orange is now interrupted colorful chips with peeping wood, metal and rust spots.

A fight breaks out. The shuffling feet between the fighters is creating thick dust clouds. A crowd is gathering. I can barely see what is going on but a loud pop echos. When the people scatter, the dust clears. I can now see a man hopping around on one leg. Two people run toward him. Acting as his leaning posts, they walk him out of sight.

As years glide by and we get older we reminisce on our wild days. Ma told us she knew all along what we were doing. She said, "As long as I had my cigarettes and beer, I didn't give a shit what yall was doing."

Fortunately, we moved out of Rockwell Gardens in 1988. Unfortunately, the gang activities escalated. Many of my former neighbors were not able to move out right away. Gang members began imposing a curfew on them so that drug operations would not get disturbed, after late hours. They also took over some people's apartments, forcing them to hide drugs and weapons.

In 2006, Rockwell Gardens was demolished, ending the era of one of the most violent housing projects in the country. On many days we made our stacked cell hole feel like an indoor amusement park for us. Yet, on the outside, these dangerous, makeshift prison buildings, were much more treacherous than prison.

Although Rockwell Gardens sounds pretty, there was nothing pretty about them. I personally believe that the government chose to put over a thousand hostile poverty-stricken Black families in one location as an attempt to provoke them into killing each other. But once the non-murderous crimes began costing the city too much money the mission had to be aborted. Only then did they decide to demolish the buildings.

The combining of thousands of angry residents, stacked on top of each other, with little to no income and little to no education turned into a minefield for continuous crimes. Be it directly and indirectly human lives were traumatically affected, especially children.

RAPE...

Does not only involve sex.
The traumatic occurrences,
experienced and witnessed,
added years to my youth...times ten.

VIOLENCE OF ANY KIND RAPES THE MIND!

Inspired by my memoir, *Brittle Never Broken.*

DODWINKLE AND DINGLEBERRY

Pretending	**L**iving
Under	**I**n
Righteous	**A**wkward
Expectations	**R**eality

Whenever Dodwinkle and Dingleberry are in each other's company life gets extremely twisted for them. Dodwinkle believes the world is ending at any given second. Dingleberry believes life is starting anew as each second passes. Neither are a **PURE LIAR**.

THE HORRORS, HUMORS AND HUMILIATIONS OF DATING WITH DISABILITIES

Do people who are born with a disability have a harder time getting dates than those who acquire a disability later in life? Since I could not find any studies to verify this comparison we may never know. However, I have interviewed several people who were either born disabled or acquired a disability, and they all share a myriad of stories that consist of either horror, humor, humiliation or all of the above.

For the sake of confidentiality, the following heterosexual daters' names have been changed. In each scenario the person with an obvious disability goes on a date with an abled body person. Also, for the sake of those who are reading this, who may have Attention Deficit Disorder (ADD, which some consider a non-obvious disability), I have used only three dating examples in hopes of sparing you from boredom.

- Heidi was stricken with polio at a very young age, and is in a wheelchair. She says throughout her dinner date her "gentleman-caller" never alluded to the fact that she was in a wheelchair. Contrary to popular belief, when you're on a date, asking questions is a must, even the ones you may be uncomfortable with. How else will you know if you want to continue seeing this person? In some cases, most abled body people may be concerned with becoming, or not becoming a caretaker. That first date is the best time to find out. Since Heidi's date wasn't open enough to address her disability his avoidance makes her question his ability to be open about anything else. Like what are his real intentions for wanting to date her...creepy dude or nah?

- ❖ Diana was born with cerebral palsy and has mild, uncontrollable muscle spasms. Yet she can walk. Some Women on a first date may find it flattering to have a guy who is an attentive gentleman–holding the door, pulling out the chair, pushing in the chair, etc. But what if he constantly jumps up from his seat to put your napkin on your lap, to slice your meat, to wipe your mouth with his napkin... Diana says she began praying that he didn't try to feed her or offer to help her pee when she excused herself to go to the bathroom. Perhaps this dude wasn't really looking for a date but for a position as a caretaker.

- ❖ Steve was in a terrible motorcycle accident, which caused him to become quadriplegic and mobile by wheelchair. His way of getting dates is quite unique. Some people may be aware of how some men like to pull the sympathy card–also known as manipulation–to get a Woman to give in to him. Steve does this regularly by pretending to be the masculine version of a damsel in distress–a damoiseau in distress I believe–in order to get what some refer to as "sympathy pussy." And for those who are wondering if his joint still works, FYI there are penis pumps for limp dicks. Anyway, Steve drops an item and pretends to struggle to pick it up. The female of his interest sees this and picks it up for him. Not only does he enjoy a great view of her back side as she bends to pick up his thrown...I mean dropped item, but as she hands it to him he gives her detailed instructions as to where she can place the item – in a zipped pouch, conveniently strapped around his waist, leaning against his penis. By the way, the pouch is overstuffed intentionally. Making it difficult to unzip and zip it back. Thus, allowing him even more time to discuss, with his unsuspecting victim...I mean future date, his long, drawn out, sob story of how a horrible accident caused him to be confined to the wheelchair. He gets her number, and the rest is history. Talk about shameless creativity.

Whether you consider these scenarios horrible, humorous, humiliating, or all of the above they all have one thing in common– the desire for companionship. You must date to find your soul mate.

What I'm really fascinated to find out is, how does a person with Tourette syndrome, who has the tic of blurting out inappropriate words, fair on dates?

A few words from the wise. Whether a person is born with a disability or acquires it later does not mean they are incapable of fully functioning. It simply means that certain body parts may be incapable of functioning at full capacity. Yes, they can still have sex. Some may require being more creative to get the job done properly.

You should also be aware that of all of the communities that are listed in society the disabled community is the one that anyone, at any time, may become a part of.

With that said remember always show everyone a lottaluv!

Be kind always!

It's really that simple.

HALF ASS GESTURE

Salivating at the prospect of his next lick
The excitement of what he can greedily take and sneakily get
Stealing hearts and minds of the unsuspecting kind
Offering flattering rendezvous with cheap wine
She's disappointed but smiles nonetheless
Feigning appreciativeness
Figuring he's done his best
He knows she has the nice girl syndrome and won't make a fuss
Merely glad for the half ass attention–a date with a hairy chest
It's the least he could do in exchange for what he'll gain
Ninety percent of her hard-earned savings
and watching her go insane
Little does he know the red flags she has noticed much
So, this half ass gesture won't suffice long enough
To steal nothing from her let alone her heart in love

MILITARY TERROR – VIETNAM 1970

I drop my heavy, triple sized duffel bag beside the flimsy-looking cot I was assigned to sleep on. I see why they're expecting to recruit physically fit guys. If a fat man ever sits on this joke-for-a-bed, it's falling to the floor and looking like a sleeping bag.

I look around this joint in total disbelief. Ha...I call my house oversized sticks barely glued together. My home is a mansion compared to this shit...an oversized outhouse. I bet them honkie's barracks lookin' like the fuckin' white house.

I sit on the cot, rubbing my forehead. From my side vision I spot a shadow on the floor. I look up at the figure it's connected with. Some skin head racist lookin' muthafucka.

With his lips barley parting he says, "Why are you in here?"

Not only has his presence pissed me off. He asks a dumb ass question as if I'd want to be sitting on someone else's concrete feeling ass cot. I suppose I didn't respond fast enough. He talks again. "I'm just saying...all the other niggers are still outside."

I stare him down as Islowly rise from the cot.

He continues running his mouth. "Oh...so you actually think your standing is supposed to frighten me, nigger?"

He walks toward me, so close his nose is almost touching mine. I don't move. He smells like my neighbor's dog's fur after he's been caught in the rain. I clench my fists. Ready to knock this muthafucka unconscious when someone grabs me around the neck from behind. His forearm pressing on my throat so hard I can't breathe. I can't move, speak or even swallow my spit.

The racist bastard gets back in my face. "From here on out you're not just a nigger to me. You're my nigger bitch. And it's not just because I'm telling you, it's because I'm going to show you."

He punches me in the stomach. I drop to the floor. I swing my elbow backward in hopes of landing it into his stomach but he dropped on top of me, gripping my neck tighter. As I'm clawing his arm, jerking and tugging to get loose, his body slams me on my stomach, pressing my face to the floor.

I see a pair of shoes. Then I feel someone tug at my belt. I fight harder to get loose. My pants are snatched to my feet. Something is pushed into my rectum, causing excruciating pain. It feels as if fire is streaming down my legs and up my back. I scream. He shoves my face harder into the ground.

He lets me go and I hear shoes scrambling. I thought I wanted to know who did this, but I'm relieved I don't have to face anyone, right now. Paralyzed more from shock than pain. Too numb to feel anything, except excretion or blood or both oozing from my rectum.

I hear voices approaching near the door but I can't make out what's being said. I manage to crawl to the cot, pulling my pants over my ass as I climb into bed. I hear someone walk in. They're somewhere behind me, so I bawl tightly into a fetal position, hugging my knees so if they're here to fuck me again they'll have to pry each of my limbs open with the jaws of life to succeed.

The footsteps get closer. A voice says my name. "Jared...is that you?"

I don't respond. He walks around to face me but I can only see the lower half of his body. He bends at the knees to look me in the face. He speaks again. "Hey man...What's going on with you? Why are you lying in bed like this?"

It's Thomas. Why is he risking being seen in here?

Although they try to make us look as if we're not segregated, it's an unspoken rule that whites don't go into an all-black barrack. And blacks know it's a possible write up, for any fucking reason, just short of a military lynching, if one of our black asses are caught in one of their barracks. But all I could say is, "I don't feel goo..."

I could barely finish my sentence when he chimes in. "I can walk with you to the infirmary." I tense tighter into my fetal position.

He sits at the foot of the cot and says, "Well tell me what you want me to do?"

If I didn't know any better, I'd swear Thomas has a smirk on his face. I close my eyes. I tell him, "I need to sleep." I feel a tear trickle along the bridge of my nose, onto the other eye. I hope Thomas didn't see it.

He stands up and asks, "You want me to bring you something–water, food, *paaain meds*?"

I open my eyes to look him in the eyes...wondering why he stressed "pain" like that? I want so badly to say, *sure how bout you give me the color of your skin so I won't have, to continue getting fucked every which way possible that the white man can think of.*

Instead, I close my eyes again and respond by shaking my head. The sound of my head moving along the pillow is like sandpaper against concrete, sending a horrible chill through my body.

Sexual Violence Remains Pervasive
Over ***1 in 4 women*** *and* ***1 in 3 men*** *were assaulted by someone in their chain of command.*
Vast Majority of Cases Go Un-Reported
If you or someone you know is a victim of rape the following resources may be helpful.

RAPE HOTLINE FOR MILITARY SERVICE PERSONS

www.protectourdefenders.com

• **14,900** *members (8,600 women and 6,300 men) were sexually assaulted in. Rates of penetrative assault were unchanged from.*

• *Most victims were sexually assaulted more than once, resulting in over* **41,000** *assaults in alone.*

• **81%** *of victims did* **not** *report the crime in.*

Retaliation Is the Norm

• ***58% of women*** *and* ***60% of men*** *who reported a sexual assault face retaliation.*

Sexual Assault is More Common in a Military Context

• In 2014, *rates were* **50%** *higher among active-duty women, and over* **100%** *higher among men, than in the*

RAPE HOTLINE FOR CIVILIANS

RAINN (Rape, Abuse & Incest National Network) is the nation's largest anti-sexual violence organization. RAINN created and operates the National Sexual Assault Hotline (800.656. HOPE, online.rainn.org y rainn.org/es) in partnership with more than 1,000 local sexual assault service providers across the country and operates the DoD Safe Helpline for the Department of Defense. RAINN also carries out programs to prevent sexual violence, help survivors, and ensure that perpetrators are brought to justice.

ASSUMPTION VS JUDGEMENT

Assumption and Judgement are the same
Though spelled differently
Resemblance in the name
An ugly hard to lose
Many are guilty and don't even choose
Assuming that person in a wheelchair
Needs or even desires your help
As opposed to preferring to do it they-self
That self-proclaimed feminist driving an eighteen-wheeler
Still wants to be treated as a lady by (wo)men who are feelin' her.

MENTAL MAYHEM

(Based on actual events)

First off, let's start by eliminating the term soccer mom. Not everyone taking their child(ren) to a sporting event is going to a soccer game. I am a proud tennis mom and will continue to refer to myself as such, even way after tennis season has ended and my daughter stops playing.

I have endured the tortures of having chatty, giggly, teenaged girls in my truck for too many tennis practices and matches. In many cases the five minutes to the park for practices seems just as long as the half hour to forty-five-minute-long drive to a match, especially when all you long for is peace and quiet. It's worse when they want you to engage in their strange conversations. I honestly could care less about the Cheetah Girls' episodes. Nor do I want to hear another radio replay of Crank That by Soulja Boy. Then there's the continuous repeat of a line from Eddie Murphy's Norbit movie, "Resputia...You know you no belong in here." I don't know how, after the 32nd time of quoting this, they still laugh as if it is their first time hearing it? So, as to not come off as bored out of my wits and nonchalant (and that's the clean version) I feign over the top elation and engage in those, energy filled, teenaged topics.

In the meantime, my mom, whose schizophrenic tendencies are starting to re-surface, has decided, a week ago, that she no longer needs to continue taking her medications. What does this mean for me? Much bigger problems than chatty, giggly teens.

Although mom is still able to function, and make sensible decisions, this week, it'll get progressively worse in another week. "Why won't you take your medicines?" I ask her. She replies, "I don't need to. I'm fine." Why was I even expecting a rational answer? Her choice has been made. Now on comes the consequences. I'm thinking maybe mom is feeling left out since I am not able to be with her as much during tennis season. And every time I ask her to come along her answer is always no. But I'm not sad about this, too much, because if she is around these strange teens, she will find a way to embarrass us all.

Being the youngest of three siblings I never would have thought that I would be the one responsible for my mother's care, in her ailing age. Not so much because of my position in the family, but because I was born with a disability myself, osteogenesis imperfect (brittle bones). I rely mostly on a wheelchair for mobility–sometimes crutches. As a result, my mother had to take an extended moment of her life to care for me in my childhood. But the tables eventually turned.

As a young adult, my mother was diagnosed with paranoid schizophrenia, manic depression. With proper medication she was able to function in her daily routine. However, it is when she gets the idea that she no longer needs her meds, and stops taking them is what creates a chaotic situation for her, and for those of us who love her.

The very first time I witnessed her ceasing to take her meds was when I was a teen. As a result, I had to stay with relatives for two weeks, until my mother was discharged from the psychiatric hospital. To me this was a horrible thing to have to temporarily live with relatives whose daily routines were far from what I was used to.

However, now I feel having my mother living in my home with my family, and watching her go through psychotic episodes, actually feels much worse, than when I was a teen battling this situation alone.

Before my husband and I brought a house, I asked him if it would be okay if my mother can live with us. I figured this is a win-win situation because my mother was on a fixed income, so a small portion of her check could cover utilities. This would be much less than the rent she

would pay in her own place. In turn, we would have someone to help us out by looking after the house while we worked. Plus, mom's home cooked meals spared me the grueling task of cooking after coming home, exhausted from working 10 hours a day–actually more than eleven hours, including traveling both ways.

But the best part is my mother and I become hanging buddies. Whenever she had a doctor's appointment, I drove her there. When we went shopping for groceries and clothing, we were together. But it gets even better when my husband and I decide to start a family. We have a healthy baby girl and thankfully mom becomes our live-in nanny.

Prior to the baby's arrival, we were able to have the basement of our home remodeled so that mom could live in a comfortable garden-like apartment. When it was time for us to leave for work my husband would take our baby downstairs to my mom and all was smooth sailing. This worked well for years. That is, until my mom again decided she no longer needed to take her medication.

The most difficult part about dealing with a person who has a mental illness is trying to convince them that their reality is not what is really happening. Although my mother stopped taking her meds on several occasions, and was committed into a psychiatric hospital, the last and almost fatal event was the worst.

I first noticed something wasn't right when mom would make comments, accusing the neighbors of watching our house, and plotting to hurt us. We have never met those people, mind you. As a matter of fact, we have only personally spoken with three of our neighbors, so those are the only few whose names we know.

But when I question my mom if she has been taking her meds she responded, belligerently, "Yes. I take my meds!" However, I did not realize she was actually only referring to all of her other meds, for high blood pressure, diabetes, blood thinner, etc. When I am specific in stating the meds for her mental condition, she avoids answering the question. That's when I knew we were heading toward trouble.

As days go by her paranoia gets worse. She would sit on the front lawn to watch the neighbors across the street.

One evening my daughter, mom and I were home. Mom comes upstairs. My daughter was in her bedroom and I was in my bedroom. She sits on my bed and begins talking about how dangerous the neighbors were because they were watching everything we were doing. Of course, I am trying to convince her otherwise, but to no avail.

As we continue talking, I notice that at the mid-front of her shirt, just above her breast, there is a pointy spot, causing her shirt to look warped. It looked as if it was hung on a hook for too long. At first, I think nothing of it, because my clothes have gotten distorted from sitting the wrong way on wire hangers. But the more I stared at the point in her shirt I concluded that if it were just from a hanger distortion, it should still be lying against her chest not suspended above it.

As she continues rattling on about her distrust of the neighbors, I work up the nerve to interrupt her and ask, “Why is your shirt so pointy above your breast?” She replies. “I have a knife in case the neighbors try to come in here.” My thoughts run wild. What if her schizophrenia gets mixed with her paranoia? In *her* mind I may become the one in cahoots with our evil neighbors. My heart is beating through my back, but I manage to stay calm. I *tell* her in an *askingly* way. “Take the knife from your chest. If you slip and fall you could stab yourself in the face.” She responds. “Pfft…I’m not gonna fall.”

My honest concerns are less about her falling, but more of her possibly choosing to mutilate my daughter and me. We sit in silence for too long. I intentionally do not keep the conversation going because I do not want to agitate her. And I am hoping if I stop responding to her accusations, she will go back downstairs. Eventually she does.

After pondering a few minutes on what I should do, I decided to call uncles, cousins, and siblings. Everyone called mom in hopes of convincing her to take her meds but they only pissed her off. I decided to call the police department. They said that there is nothing they can do since she is not directly threatening to harm anyone or herself. They suggest I contact the National Alliance for Mental Illness (NAMI).

The NAMI rep was very compassionate and understanding of my situation. However, they confirmed what I already knew–that no one can make a person take their meds, or get psychiatric help.

After talking with them a bit longer we concluded that if I call the police back, and tell them I am afraid that mom will possibly hurt me and my daughter, or even herself then they would have to come out.

It works. Two officers arrive. I explain to them that I really don't feel that she will hurt us but that she may hurt herself because the knife is in her bosom. I ask if they wouldn't mind going downstairs to talk her into removing the knife from her chest. They agree.

As they descend the stairs, they announce their presence. I tell them that her bedroom is at the back. They knock on her bedroom door and ask her to come out. But she refused. They tell her they are coming in. But when they try to open the door it's locked. I can hear what's going on so I yell down. "There is no lock on her door. How can it be locked?" They respond. "Perhaps she has something wedged under the doorknob." They ask me. "Is there a drawer with more knives?" I tell them, "Check the drawer next to the refrigerator."

They come back up with all of the remaining knives and place them on my kitchen table. They said this is the best they could do to insure us a little safety. They then wish me the best and bid me good night.

They leave and I'm still in fear for all of our lives. All this has done was defy my mother's trust in me and convince her that I too was like the scheming neighbors. From this day on instead of coming up to talk to me she starts calling me on the phone.

By now my daughter is 11 years old. Although she is aware of her granny's mental illness, I still feel the need to explain why her granny is acting strangely. She adores her granny and is a smart kid so she understands. Some years prior my daughter asked me, "Who is going to take care of me if something happens to granny, since you have to work?" My heart was crushed. I tell her, "You don't have that to ever worry about." I said this with more assurance than I felt.

Perhaps my daughter saw more of what was coming than I did. But as I assured her, I literally got my break when I fractured my hip again. This may sound strange because no one would find breaking anything as a "good" break, especially me, since I've broken so many bones. But this time re-fracturing my hip, which already had a pin in it, helped me. I was in so much pain but because the pin held the bone in place there was no need for me to be placed in a hip spica cast. So as long as I took pain pills, I was still able to get things done. Resting in spurts throughout the day was a requirement.

This time the bone took eight months to heal as opposed to the usual eight weeks. I was on medical leave waiting to heal, trying to get my mom proper mental health care and making sure my daughter's life functioned as normal as possible. But thankfully being on medical leave

made this all possible. Unfortunately, my being home, still could not prevent my mom from harming herself.

It was a Saturday. My normal routine is to wake up early but stay in bed to pray, read and meditate. One sound that I am used to hearing in the morning is my mom stirring about in the basement, fixing herself breakfast. Since she's diabetic she's usually up no later than 7:00 a.m. Sometimes she gets up, eats and goes back to lie down. The silence in the basement crosses my thoughts but it doesn't overly concern me. I drift off to sleep and awaken again around 10:00 a.m. My daughter and one of her female cousins are awake, and playing video games in the living room.

I go to ask them have they been downstairs or has granny come up? They say no. I call my mom. No answer. I don't panic, figuring she may be in the bathroom. I wait a half an hour and try calling again. Still no answer. I send my daughter and niece to check on her. When they return, they say that her door is locked and she wasn't responding to their knocks.

Now I'm panicking. I tell my husband. He goes down to check. He can't get into her bedroom so he removes the hinges from the door. He runs back up to tell me she's not waking up. I use my crutches to walk downstairs. I notice she wrapped sheets tightly around the doorknob and the dresser handle which was just as firm as a door's lock.

I stand next to her bed. When I yell her name she groggily says, "Yeah." But she never opens her eyes and goes right back into a deep sleep. I'm thinking maybe it's a diabetic coma. I call the paramedics. They come to take her to the hospital.

Tests concluded that she overdosed on her medications. They encourage me to find out which one so that they can determine how to treat her. Since the hospital isn't far from my home I go back to my mom's bedroom. I find a bottle of Seroquel lying under her bed. I take it back to the emergency room.

The doctor explained that since Seroquel is a med that they were unable to flush from her system, mom will have to sleep it off. He adds it is possible that sometime during her comatose state, she may have seizures. In some cases, patients who have seizures after overdosing on Seroquel could possibly go into cardiac arrest. He asks me, "If her heart stops would you want us to resuscitate her?" I am stunned at the question. How do I answer this? My mom has made it known many times that she is unhappy with living? I hesitate longer than I should have. Thankfully my older cousin was there to help me. She says, "Yes." Although the doctor heard her, he wanted me to answer. I repeated her yes. I then had to sign consent papers.

During the night I received a call that my mom had pretty bad seizures, several times, but they got it under control, so she should be fine. This would be the beginning of much rehab for her.

Between going to the hospital to visit my mom, then going to the clinic for myself, for the prognosis of my fractured hip and seeing to it that my daughter's homework and playtime stays balanced, I still manage to make all our lives maintain some level of normalcy.

Mental illness makes people very uncomfortable.
That's why they do not know how to treat you.

I DO NOT	**I DO WISH**
want to be	there was
responsible	a way to
for *helping*	*permanently*
you put	balance that
yourself	chemical
into a grave.	imbalance!

You knowingly and unknowingly want to die.
Repeatedly attempting to make it happen.

THE VOICE

Jocelyn leaps across the hoods and roofs of parked cars, with bare, muddy feet. A driver sitting in his car opens his door to cuss her out, but she is already two cars behind him. Just as she jumps onto the hood of the fourth car, it begins pouring down raining. She leaps onto the fifth car and slips, rolling onto the street. She jumps from the ground and steps between two parked cars, just as an eighteen-wheeler truck whizzes by her.

The rain is slowing to a drizzle. She looks around to get an idea of where she is–at the curb, in front of the neighborhood park. Across the street is a gas station. Directly in front of it, three guys are at the bus stop, rapping and dancing to their own beat.

Stepping onto the curb, Jocelyn walks toward a tree and leans against it. She looks down at herself and sees splotches of mud smeared in various places on her cream-colored, sundress.

She pulls her shoulder pouch to the front of her, takes out a cigarette and lights it. Taking a long pull, hoping to calm the voice in her head, only makes it whisper. "*Now that you've mastered walking along cars, it's time to climb to the top of trees.*" Jocelyn stares at a centipede as it wiggles its way across the grass near her foot. The voice becomes louder. *You do know that used to be you!* She exhales smoke, as she watches a couple walk by. She wonders if the voice is referring to the centipede or the couple.

As she gazes at the couple, tears sting her eyes as she reminisces on how she and Charles were once happily married, and what felt like in love. She was the envy of many Women as they watched her and Charles walk hip to hip, holding each other tightly, whenever they'd leave a live play, dinner, or the skating rink.

After their twin sons were born their love seemed to increase tenfold for each other and their boys. They lived in a big beautiful five-bedroom home with a huge backyard which Charles transformed into a playground, once the boys turned toddlers. She would prepare dinner before Charles returned from work, periodically checking on the boys, as they ran around the backyard, torturing each other. She told Charles the swing and sliding board was a waste of money, as the boys got more enjoyment wrestling in the grass or climbing the tree or fence. She especially misses making love to Charles in front of the fire place in their bedroom. She loved how he made her feel. She enjoyed making him feel good as she recalls reaching between their bodies to gently stroke his balls with one hand and lightly slide her fingernails across his back with the other hand. After almost an hour of love making, and dehydrating from all the orgasms she could take, she'd whisper the words she knew guaranteed Charles would explode. "Mmmm Chuck...You're the best fuck! Fuuuuck me...Chuuuuck!"

Jocelyn is grinning to herself when her thoughts are interrupted by an elderly lady, about two feet from her, bending over to pick up her dog's poop, with a plastic bag. Jocelyn flicks her cigarette butt into the street.

Another voice instructs her, "*Get your cell phone out your purse... call dumbass.*" She dials her cousin, Peter, who goes by the street name Cold-Pe. It goes to voicemail. Jocelyn re-dials.

Cold-Pe picks up on the first ring. "Who dis is?" Rap music blares in the background.

Jocelyn begins bouncing to the music and talking in rap form with the beat. "Heeeeey cousin Peter. God is still counting your wrong doings. You need to repent for all those murders you still walkin' free on. Oh, and while you're at it lose that dumbass name referring to yo killings."

Cold-Pe turns the music down. "Da fuck? Look i'on know what da fuck you talkin' bout...or who da fuck dis is...but I do know you bet not call my phone with dis prank ass bullshit no mo!" Click!

Jocelyn scrolls through her contacts again waiting for the voice to tell her who to call next. She dials her niece, Tammy, who she happened to see the other day driving by her, as Jocelyn was walking down the sidewalk, heading nowhere as usual. Jocelyn is about to hang up when Tammy picks up.

"Hello." Jocelyn blurts out, "God wants you to stop selling drugs and smoking weed."

"Who the fuck is this?" Tammy yells.

Jocelyn responds. "Oh, now you wanna play stupid. Just heed the word from the Lord."

Tammy lowers her voice, purses her lips, and enunciates each word. "Let me tell you something bitch...don't call my muthafuckin phone no mo. As a matter fact lose my muthafuckin number and go somewhere and die!" Tammy hangs up.

Those four words, *go somewhere and die,* continue echoing in Jocelyn's head. They are the same words that the voice says to her daily. Jocelyn takes this as confirmation as to what she should do next as she starts walking toward the street. Her eyes are fixed in the direction ahead. She can hear people yelling at her to get out of the street but she cannot control herself. Go *somewhere and die.* The light turns green as she steps into the first lane of five lanes of oncoming traffic. Go *somewhere and die.* Two lanes flow in one direction, heading westbound. In the middle lane cars are turning left. The other two lanes head eastbound. Go *somewhere and die.*

Jocelyn makes it safely across two lanes as cars are blowing and brakes are screeching. Go *somewhere and die.* She sees people at the bus stop gesturing and yelling for her to get out of the street. Go *somewhere and die.* She steps into the turn lane.

A driver hits the brakes but still slams directly into her.

She flies into the air, flips several times over the top of the car. Her body thumps onto the ground. She lands on her side, near the driver's back tire.

When the left arrow turns green. The driver slams the accelerator, running over Jocelyn's left leg. Jocelyn slowly slides her arm near her face. She lifts her shoulders and body slightly from the ground. Go *somewhere and die.* She slumps back down.

Drivers pull over, jump out of their cars and go where Jocelyn lies. Several pedestrians surround her, as many continue coming. One man quickly opens Jocelyn's purse. Without even seeing what the contents are he grabs everything out with one hand and stuffs them into his pocket. A bystander notices but says nothing.

Another gentleman kneels beside her to check her pulse. He asks, "Are you able to talk? If you can hear me move your right hand." There is no response.

NAMI, the National Alliance on Mental Illness, is the nation's largest grassroots mental health organization dedicated to building better lives for the millions of Americans affected by mental illness. If you or someone you know are in need:

Find Help in a crisis

www.nami.org/Home

CALL EMAIL OR TEXT

THE NAMI HELPLINE

Monday-Friday, 10 AM - 6 PM ET

(800) 950-NAMI(6264)

info@nami.org

or Text "NAMI" to 741741

DRIVE YOURSELF SANE

I enjoy my second job as a dog sitter.
They can't speak human language.
Or can they?
Even though their growl is scary sometimes, it's merely a warning.
You walk away.
Their growl fades.
But with certain people, too many of them are so unpredictable
and downright
Fucking evil.
To the point of being deeply Satan possessed.
So, of course, these demonic occurrences happen at my main work as a
Domestic Violence Advocate.
One guy sets his lady on fire while she's at a daycare.
Another guy stuffs mixed concrete into his girlfriend's vagina,
after he strangles her to
Death, then watches the concrete dry and swell inside her.
Whelp...at least she didn't feel the pain of her vagina exploding
and pelvis shattering.
My current client says her boyfriend, not her husband,
not even her fiancé, not that it
Would've made a difference as to their relationship,
but her so called boyfriend put a
Loaded gun to her head, and told her to exit his car
while driving, at least, 65 miles per hour on the expressway.
I truly do not understand why that misogynistic,
snake twin isn't on death row awaiting
Six hundred and sixty-six electric chairs
Or worse consecutive life sentences!

DOUGH BOY

When Byron pulls up in his maroon Cadillac Allanté my mouth drops. His boy, Marley pulls right behind him in another black one. I really should close my mouth.

I got a thing for Marley so I walk over to his car and rub the hood. Marley rolls down the passenger side window and asks, "You wanna take a spin?"

Oh my God, he wants me to sit next to him. I get to actually breath in his carbon dioxide. Well actually I got some better ideas for the type of spinning I'd rather take with him...but instead I say, "I don't know. This may be a little too luxurious for me."

He scuffs. "Too luxurious for you? Who says that? Get in."

I sit down and place my crutches in the space between the door and my seat. I want to say so much to him about him but instead I say, "Woooow! It's gorgeous in here! Leather everything! Okay now these seats are a bit too low. I can't even see over the dashboard." I sneakily lift my butt to sit on my purse.

Marley looks at me. I hope he didn't notice. "So, you not feelin the bucket seats huh?" Marley asks.

Oh no he saw me. I respond with a dry, "Naaaa."

He grins and says, "You ready? Fasten your seat belt."

The tires screech as he pulls off, speeding toward Central Avenue. I grab the door handle and lean further into the back of the seat. We take a turn onto North Avenue, speeding down to Cicero, back over to Division and up to Laramie and back to LeMoyne. If it weren't for the stop lights, making us have to stop, I would've shit and piss my pants.

He parks in the same spot. I thank him but sit for a few seconds. Wishing hard he'd lean over to kiss me. Instead he says, "You weren't scared, were you?" He smirks. Oh my God those pretty white teeth embedded between those thick, smooth, bright, pink lips. The brightest I've ever seen on a dark-skinned dude. His eyes slant so thinly, making him look blackanese–Black mixed with Chinese.

I smile and respond, "Pfft...Of course not."

He busts up laughing. Okay maybe now he's going to kiss me. Instead he says, "Well I gotta make a run. Maybe we'll do this again another time."

I wanna say yeah right. Instead, I hump my shoulders, trying to appear nonchalant and say, "Okay" as I open the car door.

There are more people here standing around than it was when I left. Byron's arms are folded as he leans his back against his driver side door. I slip into the passenger side seat, and yell toward him. "Hey Byron! Take me for a spin!"

He looks down into the car, chuckling. "Whatcho' li' butt doin' in here?"

I smile. He responds, "A'right give me a minute." He stands upright again, continues talking. I turn the volume up on the radio, singing along with White Horse by Laid Back. "If you wanna ride...Don't ride the white horse...White horse...Don't ride the white horse..." The music plays before the next verse begins, "If you wanna be rich, you got to be a bitch."

Byron reaches inside the window, turns the volume even louder. He sings the verse louder than the song. "If you wanna be rich, you got to be a bitch!" He looks at me. We both bust up laughing.

He then opens the door and jumps in. "I gotta pick up a package right quick. Fasten yo seat beat. Don't want yo' lil ass flyin' through the windshield if I have to stop real fast." He busts up laughing at his own visual. I smaile. He revs the motor. The tires screech when he pulls off. Talking about me flying out if he stops, he's gonna cause injuries just pulling off.

Everybody's staring at us. We come to a stop light. The dude in the car, next to us, does the cordial head nod. Byron does it back. The light turns green and Byron peels off again. We're swerving in and out of lanes.

We arrive in an area I've never seen. As Byron slows down, he turns the radio down. We can no longer see the street from here. The headlights make it possible to see mounds of garbage piled two stories high. This seems to go on for blocks. Once we stop completely, Byron looks swiftly from the rearview to the side view mirror, then through his window and mine, then back out the rearview mirror.

I see a car slowly pull up behind us. Byron looks out his side view mirror. Some guy walks up. Byron speaks firmly to the guy. "Hey! Maaaan. I tol' cho ass don't be talkin' all that shit on da phone. You gone make me think some funny shit bout yo' ass. If da heat come at me it's yo' ass. Pull that shit again and Imma have to fuck ya up! Where my dough...boy?"

The guy snaps. "Hey! Watch that *boy* shit!" He bends over, looks at me, then hands Byron a brown paper bag. Byron opens the bag, lifts up a wad of cash and flips through it like it's a deck of cards.

The boy asks, "That's yo' Woman?"

Byron peeks swiftly into the rearview mirror. "Naw man...That's my cousin." They start talking some jargon I have no clue about.

The boy starts again with his personal opinion. "Yo cousin my ass!"

Byron snaps. "Man! Get da fuck away from my car."

The boy takes a step backward.

Byron puts the car in drive. As he slowly pulls off, he yells out. "I'll letchu know where I'll be next."

The boy yells back. "Yeah whateva! I know that's yo damn Woman!"

Byron speeds off and starts again gazing longer into his rear and side view mirrors. Now I'm checking my side view mirror more often. It looks like the same car is still behind us. We turn so many S curves, it's like a maze. It seems to get even more darker, despite the headlights shining. Byron flicks on the bright lights. I stare at him as he takes both hands off the steering wheel, and lifts his body to shove the brown paper bag down his crouch. He bucks his eyes toward me and gets smart. "Dang! You lookin fa sumin?"

I bust up laughing. He chuckles. I ask, "You done got lost in this dump?"

He doesn't respond. Too engrossed in checking his mirrors. I check my mirror. The car is no longer behind us. It's now pure darkness. Finally, I see cars going by at the cross section ahead. For a few seconds, I'm embarrassed with myself for feeling this giddy about seeing street lights.

We're driving down Pulaski. So many people standing around, especially near the liquor stores. Byron blasts the music again. L.L. Cool J's song I'm Bad is playing. Byron starts rapping along:

...I'm as strong as bull of course you know I am pull
I enjoy what I'm doing plus I'm paid in full
Not Buckaroo Bonsai but busted out as I
Say the kind of rhymes that make MC's wish that I die...

As we turn down North Avenue, we're both bouncing to the beat. Byron is still nervously checking the side and rear-view mirrors but doesn't miss a beat with the lyrics. I check the side view mirror. I rap in snippets to the parts I know. I definitely know the I'm Bad part.

The sirens blare through the speakers confusing me because it sounds like the cops are actually driving near us. I even turn to look out the back window just to make sure. We come to a stop light.

The driver on my side smiles and bobs his head with us. I'm enjoying the attention. I look at Byron. He stops rapping. His eyes grow big as he yells. "GET DOWN!" Instead of ducking I turn to look out the window to see what he's looking at. I don't get a chance to because he throws the car in reverse. We're speeding down the center lane.

CAPTURED

It's mid-term week of my sophomore year in high school, and I'm enjoying everything but algebra. I stay late after school, in my math tutoring class. When I get home, after eating dinner I go online to get more help with figuring out more algebra problems. This goes on well into the wee hours of the night, and I still can't seem to grasp this crap.

I'm right back up, a few hours later, starting another long day. The exhaustion is weighing heavier on me this morning, more than all other days. The gloomy morning, due to the pouring rain, is adding to the heavy feeling in my legs. My feet feel as if I'm dragging twenty pounds of cement, as I slog my body to the El station. While sitting on the platform bench, I pull out math notes to study some more.

I hear the train approaching, so I stuff my papers into my backpack. From my side view, I see a man running down the steps. I figured he's rushing to catch the train. But he stops right in front of me and punches me in the face.

Jocelyn is about to fall when another man standing behind her catches her limp body, turns her toward him, places his lips against her lips, giving passersby the impression that they're kissing. A few people exit the train and continue walking swiftly to their destinations. The two men hold Jocelyn's limp body up between them, then walk unto the train and sit down. Only one other person is on the train but he has on headphones, bobbing his head.

*****

When I wake up, I'm lying on a mattress, in a cage. One of my wrists is strapped to a bed's headboard. I reach with my free hand to try to slide my cuffed hand out. When that doesn't work, I yank hard, causing a surge of pain through my entire arm. Although my face is throbbing, all I can think about is that I'm missing my math test. There goes passing that class.

A frail, pale, white dude, with red thinning hair, walks in with a plate of food. He speaks gently. "I have a sandwich here for you beautiful." As he approaches the cage, my eyes follow his movements. He removes the lock. Walks in, sits on the mattress, still grasping the plate. He lies the plate on the mattress and says, "My name is Roger but everyone around here calls me Ro." I wonder who is everyone? He continues. "I know you're afraid...being in a strange and scary looking place and all, but it's really not that bad in here. The reason you're here...like...this...is because we want to help you. I know your family is struggling, y'all being poor and all...and we want to help you make money...So we want to do better by you and your family."

I want to kick him in the teeth, for even thinking I would believe this bullshit. He goes on. "This is the fastest and easiest way to make money, but I must remind you as long as you cooperate there will be no problems. No one will get hurt or even killed if you do right by us. So, this verbal agreement will be official with your verbal answer of yes."

I nod my head.

He closes his eyes. "Well apparently...you didn't understand. So, let me make myself clearer. A verbal agreement is when words are exchanged, not gestures. Well maybe I'll back track here. Your name is Jocelyn Merrigole. Your mother, father and brother are Terana, Matthew and Jonathan. I know where you all live. Correction... where *you used to live* with them. And of course, I know where you *went* to school." Leaning closer to look Jocelyn directly in the eyes, he emphasizes, "I've even seen all of your cute little stuffed animals along the wall on your tiny bed...Joc. Yep I even know that's your precious pet name your family calls you."

My eyes sting with tears. I abruptly turn my head. He grabs my chin and snatches my face back towards him. "If you *do not* cooperate you murder all three of your family members. I really would hate to see your best friend and baby brother be taken away from you. After all who else can you turn to when your dad goes into a drunken stupor and beats your mom? Now that I've made myself extremely clear let's clear up more terms of this verbal agreement. Your new name is Jaybird. Your job title is *tollway tinder.* You'll be trained in your duties by the other girl tinders soon, but you're a smart girl so I'm confident you'll catch on quick. You will keep your mouth closed about your job. Your duty is to complete each task as joyously as possible so that your clients will have sincere happy endings. Any bad reports and you will reap severe repercussions from various members of our staff. Now as stated before this deal is sealed with your *verbal* agreement. In other words, I fucking need to hear you!"

I flinch and muster a shaky "Yes."

He yells, "Speak up!"

I yell back, "Yes!" Tears trickle down my cheeks.

He calms down. "Now that we're finally both in agreement...oh and don't worry I have it all recorded. Smile for the camera." He points at an area on the wall. "Now all you need to do is give me your best example of how you plan to perform for your clients, and the deal is sealed."

He starts unfastening his pants. My eyes widen then it feels as if my heart drops before the rapid heartbeats begin. I plead. "No. Please no. Is there some other way I can prove myself?"

He snatches my ankles so that I'm lying flat on the mattress.

I yell. "Noooooo...Oh God please don't!" Before mounting me, he grabs my breasts and sucks. He rams his penis inside me. I don't recognize my own voice; like several animals being roasted alive. My vagina is on fire. This would be so much more fulfilling for me if he... "Please kill me." I whisper. But the voice did not sound like mine. He looked at me as if he'd forgotten I was the reason for his filthy pleasure.

He jumps up, looks around the room disoriented before finally speaking. "Now that was good and *tinder.* You'll definitely make clients happily feel that fire." He then stumbles out the room. The *one* thing that gave me enough pride to walk around this earth with dignity is demolished...my virginity.

HUMAN TRAFFICKING RESOURCE

Human trafficking is the business of stealing freedom for profit. In some cases, traffickers trick, defraud or physically force victims into providing commercial sex. In others, victims are lied to, assaulted, threatened or manipulated into working under inhumane, illegal or otherwise unacceptable conditions. It is a multi-billion-dollar criminal industry that denies freedom to 24.9 million people around the world.

Sex trafficking is the crime of using force, fraud or coercion to induce another individual to perform commercial sex. Common types include escort services, pornography, illicit massage businesses, brothels, outdoor solicitation.

Labor trafficking is the crime of using force, fraud or coercion to induce another individual to work or provide service. Common types include agriculture, domestic work, restaurants, cleaning services, and carnivals.

Every 92 seconds, an American is sexually assaulted.
Every 9 minutes, that victim is a child.
Only 5 out of every 1,000 perpetrators will end up in prison.

If you suspect someone is a victim of human trafficking or child abuse and you do not feel comfortable contacting the police department, try contacting one or both of these resources. You may be the only one who can help save their life.

https://polarisproject.org/human-trafficking/sex-trafficking
National Human Trafficking Hotline 1 (888) 373-7888
BeFree Textline Text "BeFree" (233733)

CHILD ABUSE RESOURCE

What is child abuse? Child abuse is when a parent or caregiver, whether through action or failing to act, causes injury, death, emotional harm or risk of serious harm to a child. There are many forms of child maltreatment, including neglect, verbal abuse, physical abuse, sexual abuse, exploitation, and emotional abuse. Every year more than 3 million reports of child abuse is made in the United States.

NATIONAL CHILD ABUSE 24/7 HOTLINE
(800) 4-A-CHILD (800) 422-4453
https://www.childhelp.org/hotline/

ANOTHER'S LOVE IS UNNEEDED

You don't need a daddy's love to sincerely love others
You don't need a Mother's love to sincerely love others
You don't need another's love to sincerely love others

It's their lack of love
that should teach you how to sincerely love others.

Regardless of anyone's lack of anything
is all the more reason you should want to give more
to those who need and appreciate what you desire to give

When you love those who don't love you,
When you give to those who don't appreciate it,
When you help those, who aim to destroy you,
It's time to recharge and start anew.
Patiently wait
Seek those who can reciprocate
Who are sincerely loving,
Sincerely kind and
Sincerely helpful
Just as you are.

NUMBING OUT

My brother was born in 1962. A year later my sister was born.
Ma was embarrassed about having babies
so close in age, out of wedlock.
Once they were both walking, she convinced those
who were clueless that they were twins.
About 1967, Ma almost succeeded in jumping over a fenced barrier,
outside of her tenth-floor apartment.
Her niece grabbed her in time.
In 1968, during Ma's third pregnancy with me,
doctors diagnosed her with pre-partum depression.
After I was born, Ma's diagnosis changed to post-partum depression.
She again, attempted to murder herself by overdosing.
Her niece found her in time, again.
Ma periodically reminds all three of us siblings
how if she had known about birth controls
none of us would be here.
She even told me that she once contemplated
blowing my brains out then her own.
She was committed into several insane asylums.
Doctors labeled her paranoid schizophrenic, manic-depressive.

****

I'm only five. "Oh baby...Only God knows how much we can bear." I don't know what the hell that means! If it's not Ma sayin' it it's my aunts. Now it's the nurse. I'm so SICK of hearing this shit! I'm positive that if they were the ones breaking a femur bone, going in and out of surgery, getting pins placed in their legs, having physical therapy, being incased in casts, breaking a tibia bone, and doing it *all*, all over again, they wouldn't want to hear this shit either! Ma says when I was two years old, I fell, running through the house playing with cousins. This is when doctors *finally* diagnosed me with Osteogenesis Imperfecta (OI or brittle bones). That was the last time I walked without assistive devices. I recall having dreams of walking freely. But then I wake up still living a nightmare. Pissed off all over again, at this God who "knows how much I can bear." Ha! I can't even *bear* down too hard on my legs, without being whisked off again in *another* ambulance. *Another* trip to the emergency room reveals either *another* broken tibia, fibula, femur or hipbone.

At this point, I've been to the clinic, the hospital and the emergency room so much my medical records show that I have well over a hundred visits.

****

My brother's a homebody. We spend many fun times together–playing games, watching TV, even occasionally having civil conversations. That is, when he doesn't flip out on me for unknown reasons. My sister, on the other hand, is rarely home.

"Food ready!" Ma screams from the kitchen, which is only approximately thirty feet from the living room. She has to yell because my brother has the volume blaring on the TV as usual. I can always tell what she's cooking. Not because of what day it is, Monday, but because of the yummy aroma of stewing pork. She fixes my plate and places it on the dining table. I don't move from the couch yet because the instrumental theme song of the TV show, "M*A*S*H"1 is playing. The acronym stands for Mobile Army Surgical Hospital. Although my brother is singing all of the actual words, the only part I know I sing along with him: "*Suicide is painless. It takes on many changes and I can take or leave it if I please.*" I've only watched snippets of certain episodes. I don't get it. But my brother is engrossed in *every* episode. I watch him as he's watching it, wondering why this show is so fascinating to him? But then I decide, I really don't care.

Ma steps out onto the porch, yelling my sister's name repeatedly. My sister will probably come in after we've all gone to bed, despite it being a school night. Ma comes back in shouting again, this time directly at me. "Come on eat fo' yo' food get col'!" I go wash my hands. Then hoist my body up into the dining chair. Dinner is pig feet, pig ears, pinto beans and corn bread. My brother rushes to fix his plate when a commercial comes on. Then rushes back to the couch, pulling up a dining chair, using it as a makeshift table. He keeps turning his head to the right to watch TV. Then straight again to feed his face. It's a wonder he doesn't get a crook in his neck. Well, it would serve him right if he did, for all the bad he's done to me. One day he burned my Barbie dolls, which blackened and disfigured their body parts. Another time he colored on me and the bedroom furniture, with a red permanent marker. Somehow, he found my diary and read it, despite my pleads against it. He then taunted me about it in front of my friends. But the worst was when he punched me in the nose, making it bleed. I cried to Ma but she nonchalantly tells him, "Leave her alone."

The pig foot is sticky, with several small bones. I eat it with my hands. The pig ear has no bones, just a thin gristle sandwiched between skins, which is best eaten with a fork and knife. I flip the ear over, checking for hair. There is a cluster of hair. I scrape that off along with a big chunk of skin. Ma fusses, "You throwin' 'way the best part." I tell her she can have it. I pretend the ear is steak, elegantly slicing a portion, then gently placing it in my mouth, like how the rich white people do on TV. I dowse the beans with mounds of sugar, then smoosh the Jiffy Mix cornbread into them. I devour each pig part and ask for another ear. Ma snatches my plate, looking at it, and complaining as she walks toward the stove. "You need to finish these beans." I re-sing the "M*A*S*H" theme song loudly. "*Suicide is painless. It takes on many changes and I can take or leave...*" "Shut up! I can't hear the TV!" My brother yells. I sing softer because the song keeps replaying in my head.

****

Between the ages of five and eight, my method of mobility is scooting on my butt. The butt part of all of my pants are frayed. My hands stay caked with dirt. One weekend, when my cousin comes to visit, he brings a skateboard. I get this brilliant idea that I can ride it by sitting on it. I try to steady my body but the skateboard keeps leaning too far to one side. My cousin says that's because he loosened the wheels to glide better. He uses a butter knife as a makeshift screw driver to tighten the screws. I get back on. It's steadier. I push myself, with both palms on the floor. Gliding across the living room, I stop in the dining area. The dining and living rooms are all-in-one. The dinner table on one side of the room and the couch on the other distinguishes the areas. It's a challenge turning the skateboard around to head back in the other direction. Leaning back slightly to put more weight on my butt lifts the front so I can twirl around easier. I whoosh away again. Smiling and wishing I had one like it. This method of mobility would certainly eliminate the excruciatingly painful scrapes and foreign objects that gets lodged into my butt cheeks. I've learned to tolerate the slashes, callouses and occasional splinters on and in my hands.

Whenever I'm back in the emergency room with another broken leg it means one of several things have happened–falling, abruptly tensing up, twisting too fast, handled too roughly by another person, sneezing, etc. The uncontrollable muscle spasms, as a result of a break, makes the pain even more excruciating. I wait, for what seems like hours, for my name to be called. Once I'm called, I'm pushed into a room, only to wait some more.

A nurse touches my leg.
More pain.
A doctor pokes and prods my leg.
Even more pain.
I'm whisked off to radiology.
They transfer me unto the cold metal bed-table.
Agonizing pain.
The x-ray technician, without warning, repositions my broken leg.
The muscle spasms are overpowering.
I scream.
Tears stream excessively down my face.
When I return to the room the nurse asks,
"Do you want something for the pain?"
I tell her yeah but the pain remains.
It's like I've simply chased SweeTarts[2] candy with water.

****

My sister is seventeen years old when she tells Ma she's pregnant. I'm used to Ma yelling but this news has her tones at a piercingly high octave. "Dis yo' las' year of high school! How could you be so stupid?" I'm elated that I'll be an aunt at the age of thirteen. But I can't show it so I go to my bedroom to privately rejoice. Thus, the arguing between them begins.

After my sister graduates from high school she gets married and moves out.

****

Ma is talking off again. "Yall need to believe me when I say the mafia is after me...And be careful whatchu say on dat phone 'cause the govment is listenin' to er'thang we say...I just hope they don't cut me off Social Security." Hearing only one of these sentences is the telltale sign that she has stopped taking her meds (Thorazine) for at least two-weeks. My brother yells at her. "Aaaah...There you go talkin crazy again! If the mafia wanted-chu, you woulda been dead by now!"

Ma's staying awake, throughout the night, loudly re-playing gospel albums on the stereo. It's difficult falling asleep but I finally drift off. Only to be startled awake again by loud screaming. It's Ma declaring the holy spirit. She eventually quiets down but the music continues blaring. I have school in a few hours.

When the third week approaches, Ma is committed into another psyche-ward. I stay with my sister and her family for about two weeks. I would much rather go with Ma.

My teenage mentality transforms into a wise adult's soul.
I need to become Ma's caretaker so we
don't have to be apart, anymore.

****

My brother's in another drunken stupor. Barely able to stand up straight, but still able to bug Ma for another dollar so he can get drunker. I am so sick of another dramatic episode of him repeatedly begging, threatening to rob and kill someone, *threatening to kill himself.* Then Ma repeatedly, pleading for him to go sleep it off, shouting no with annoying explanations. That is, until she finally gives in. He staggers out to buy more to drink. I go to my bedroom and close the door but I can still hear Ma ranting, "I wish he'd care his tail to bed somewhere."

It's afternoon, the next day and my brother is still passed out in his bed. I don't know what time he got in but I *do* know his drunken routine. It doesn't matter what time he passes out, he would usually be awake by now, sitting in front of the TV. The "Cheers" theme song[3] plays without him:

Making your way in the world today takes everything you've got.
Taking a break from all your worries sure would help a lot.
Wouldn't you like to get away?

I sing along:

Sometimes you wanna go where everybody knows your name.
And they're always glad you came.
You wanna be where you can see our troubles are all the same.
You wanna be where everybody knows your name.
You wanna go where people know people are all the same.
You wanna go where everybody knows your name.

I even imitate the piano finale when I hear my brother yell something, but his words stop abruptly. He does it again. Then again. "He took my Thorazine pills last night. Poison control says he gotta sleep it off." Ma says this as if she's informing me of the weather. Although I am concerned if he'll pull through this, I'm also relieved that he can't wake up right now. He sleeps 'til nighttime.

****

My cousin invites me and Ma to a church service. I'm excited at first. But when Sunday comes, I get a bad feeling, but I brush it off. It's pouring down raining. My cousin picks us up in her car. We arrive at church. I open the door to exit the back seat. I close the door but it didn't close all the way. I turn around to seal it. Placing the palms of my hands on the door and leaning my chest on the back of my hands, I apply pressure with my upper body. The rain makes the door slippery. My entire body slides downward, but I swiftly twist myself around to avoid falling face down in the mud. I'm holding myself up with both palms of my hands. The back of my dress dangles in muddy water. My crutches lie next to me. I am usually able to pick myself up but I can't this time. Ma gets behind me, lifts me, and return me to the back seat. I can feel my right hip getting heavier. Ma asks, "You wanna go home or da hospi'." I say home. We arrive in front of our apartment building. My hip feels so weighted down it's like a brick has been implanted in it. I burst out crying and apologizing. Between uncontrollable sobs, I confess that I need to go to the hospital.

X-rays show nothing.
MRI results are negative.

The doctor explains since my bones are so dense it's difficult to locate the problem. As a last resort, I am required to drink a colored liquid. I glide through a tube-shaped tunnel called a CAT scan. Finally, the results show that I have a hair line fracture in my right pelvic bone. The doctor says I need another operation. Tears pour as I plead, "Pleeease...No more surgery!" The doctor mechanically consoles me with hollowed emotions. He then gives me two options: A) No surgery and remain in bed for about *six to eight months to heal.* Or B) Surgically insert a pin to repair the bone and wear a hip Spica cast for only *six to eight weeks.*

Of course, I opt for:

another surgery,

another pin,

another cast.

I am eighteen years old.

****

My brother is in his bedroom bench pressing weights with his friends, talking loudly and drinking. A loud pop rings throughout the apartment. One of his friends scream, "Nigga you coulda killed me!"

Not long after that incident, my brother begins wearing wrist bands. I figured it was because he lifted weights. Many years later I learn, from his wife, that he was covering scars where he sliced himself. He even video recorded his last will and testament, distributing his possessions to each family member. We found it hilarious because all he had was jewelry and a gun. He applied for a gun card and over time was able to, legally purchase five guns. I questioned him about purchasing so many guns. He said he just liked collecting them. On several occasions, he told his wife that he thought about blowing his brains out. But he didn't want her to come home from work to find him like that.

She told him he needs to stop talking crazy.

But his conversations and behavior became more erratic.

It became too unbearable for his wife.

So, she left him.

Just

in

time.

Inspired by my memoir, *Brittle Never Broken.*

The warning signs of suicide are indicators that a person may be in acute danger and may urgently need help.

- **Talking about wanting to die or to kill oneself;**
- **Looking for a way to kill oneself;**
- **Talking about feeling hopeless or having no purpose;**
- **Talking about feeling trapped or being in unbearable pain;**
- **Talking about being a burden to others;**
- **Increasing the use of alcohol or drugs;**
- **Acting anxious, agitated, or reckless;**
- **Sleeping too little or too much;**
- **Withdrawing or feeling isolated;**
- **Showing rage or talking about seeking revenge; and**
- **Displaying extreme mood swings.**

THE NATIONAL SUICIDE PREVENTION LIFELINE

Provides free and confidential emotional support to people in suicidal crisis or emotional distress 24 hours a day, 7 days a week, across the United States. The Lifeline is comprised of a national network of over 150 local crisis centers, combining custom local care and resources with national standards and best practices.

The National Suicide Prevention Lifeline is a leader in suicide prevention and mental health crisis care. Since its inception, the Lifeline has engaged in a variety of initiatives to improve crisis services and advance suicide prevention for all, including innovative public messaging, best practices in mental health, and groundbreaking partnerships.

https://suicidepreventionlifeline.org/

(800) 273-8255

Crisis Text Line 741741

THAWED

Now that I've been feelingless
I prefer that
It was so much safer
Now that you make me feel again
I fight it with fear
But at the same time
I feel like melting butter
Yay happy again
Wait nervous again
Excited about this new thing
Looking back at the pass in hopes of being rescued back into a safe zone
No one is showing up
Reinvigorated
Free
Divorced
Divorced from obligations
Divorced from misery
Divorced from doing things I loathe
Divorced from those who make me feel divorced
Now what
Enjoy it
You've never done this before
It's feeling damn good
Didn't know freedom
Could feel so damned good
Though I still have nine hundred and ninety-nine problems
Peace, Happiness and Freedom are not them.

TRADITION STOLE MY BIRTHRIGHT

Dear Family, Society, the Government and ALL powers that be,

I was never comfortable with titles: BLACK HISPANIC DISABLED FEMALE STRAIGHT GAY BISEXUAL BIRACIAL SHORT TALL FAT SKINNY POOR RICH WELL OFF. This matters too much only for those who desire to put others in a particular category. Determining their status and lifestyle solely to judge them.

I was never accepting of having wifely duties. I should not HAVE to cook, clean, do laundry, or give my body parts over to another label to enjoy even when I have no desires to do so.

I am irked with the terms "a good girl" and "that's not nice." I didn't always want to be neither of those things especially not every day and sometimes not even for a few minutes. Those terms made me fight with myself to not be true to myself to succumb to someone else's or everyone else's mood. I then adopted and projected these controlling terms onto others continuing the vicious cycle of more unwanted, restricting, irritating, inhibiting societal normal bullshyt.

I hate working a job eight hours or more a day for five, sometimes six and seven days a week to only have two days, or none to myself. Then having to sit at a desk in front of a computer during most of those hours felt like a jail sentence. One hour for lunch fifteen-minute breaks. Give me a break!

All I wanted was to do and be me and still live happily. I often say the powers that be take advantage of the needs of the people. Food water housing and clothing became controlled commodities. It is required that you work to make money to buy more and more of what we don't need or even want.

Industrialization is the original crack cocaine. Creating things faster and making them easier to access made it a need. No...more like an addiction. Exactly when did binge watching become a thing.

Don't say that. That's not ladylike (Tramp/Slut...)
Don't do that. You act like a girl (Faggot/Queer...)
Don't wear that. You look like a prostitute
(Whore/ (THOT=that hoe ova there...)

THIS IS MY BODY!
MY BRAIN TO MAKE MY OWN CHOICES!

STOP TELLING ME
HOW TO ACT
HOW TO BE
WHAT TO SAY

That time dad/grandad/uncle wanted a kiss and I refused I was told, "Don't do that to your grandpa. Give him a hug and kiss." I did as I was told under parent/guardian/grandparents/government obedience aka controllers. Now he is touching my privates and making me kiss and touch him when no one is looking. I'm too afraid to say anything because they are the ones who made me do it with him in plain sight.

People who *enjoy* controlling others continue on as if they are the solution. Though they need professional help the most it is only those who are controlled who are convinced to get professional help.

This is merely one of the repercussions of allowing tradition to rob you!

Inspired by: *Gather Together in My Name* by the late legendary Dr. Maya Angelou

Glass ceiling: An invisible barrier which keep minorities from rising above a certain level in the work world. For Women, especially Women of Color, the options are still limited.

maya angelou - Bing images

Those who suffer from low self-worth put themselves through horrible situations just to survive. Dr. Maya Angelou experience misfortunes with survival, after becoming a teenage mother. Desiring to live a better life away from the discriminating poor south she moves to California. In her mind her limited options were to find a generous man to love her, instead she became a successful pimp, prostitute, and waitress. but none were successful.

Dr. Angelou's story is typical of most Women
who lack love for themselves.
After living a life of hardship some Women tend to fantasize
about finding a man who will care for them better than they
can care for themselves, only to end up hurt and disappointed.
Some Women will put themselves through many shameful
situations to either get ahead in life, win a man's love, or both.
Dr. Angelou became a pimp and was able to make good money.
After that ended, she fell in love with a man and voluntarily
became a prostitute for him. Only because she believed that
he was in danger of losing his life due to a gambling debt.
The lack of love in childhood and/or desperation
is the result of a misguided adult.
Unable to determine what sincere love is makes it
difficult to love oneself enough to know what type
of treatment is right and what is all wrong.
However, some Women have experienced enough disappointments
and hurtful situations, due to the false belief that someone
else can love them better than they can love themselves.
When a Woman learns to sincerely love herself is when she can
stop depending on others to develop true power over her own life.

PROLOGUE

In 2007 I went on disability leave from my job. I promised myself when I healed, I would get into a career that did not feel like work. I wanted the feeling that I could not believe I was being paid for having fun. It took me eight months to heal. I prayed for answers. I thought since I love to read, I'll find a career that requires reading. But once I found that I would have to read things that I found boring that changed.

Unexpectedly, that still small voice asked, "Why do Women stay in abusive relationships?" I began researching answers to the question. The first book I found is by Patricia Evans called *Controlling People: How to Recognize, Understand, and Deal with People Who Try to Control You*. On the back cover it reads:

"Does this sound like someone you know?

- Aells you who you are and what you think
- Tells you who you are and what you think
- Implies that you're wrong or inadequate when you don't agree
- Is threatened by people who are "different"
- Feels attacked when questioned
- Doesn't seem to really hear or see you

When I took this book home, I called my husband at that time (who was at work) and read it to him. I asked him, "Who does this sound like?" Shockingly he admitted it sounded like him.

It was then that I realized that voice did not ask me the question to find out the answer for other victims' problems it was a question for my own wake-up call.

Receiving this knowledge began a long battle of learning who my husband, at the time, really was. But better still finding out who I was and how I got there. I had to re-learn how to live with a controlling husband while still maintaining my sanity, while strategizing on how to get away from the toxic environment.

There's a saying, "Be careful what you ask for because you just might get it." There is no way your life can remain the same after learning the truth. Once I was awakened to what hidden abuse, manipulation and control really was I had to change myself.

Once I began to change myself everything around me changed. I had to start a whole new life for myself. Setting boundaries is difficult when you're used to not having any. Family, relatives, and friends didn't know how to handle the new me when I learned to say no or made myself unavailable for what they wanted.

What really fascinated me was realizing that I was not alone. The more I learned about intimate partner violence (IPV) the more I realized too many people, particularly Women, are suffering due to some type of abuse.

Much of my writings stem from extensive research about abuse. Although I started out learning about IPV I found that abuse is pandemic. As of writing this book there are five types of abuse: physical, sexual, verbal, emotional/psychological and financial. Upon revising this book, I have learned that digital abuse has been added. These abuses can occur anywhere, at any time, among anybody.

Learning as much as I have about various types of abuse is why I started WEWIN-Women Empower Women in Need Queendom. WEWIN Queendom's goal is to empower Women of all races, creed, religion, and status. We provide information and various type of personal assistance and resources for Women who are in need or just need to know and have a discussion about it.

Follow me everywhere!

💝 Website: http://www.marvinasims.com/books

👑 Instagram: Instagram.com/marvina_sims

👑 WEWIN Queendom Facebook:
https://www.facebook.com/2LOVEWEWIN/

👑 YouTube Channel: https://www.youtube.com/channel/UCWPRiCH1N2KCMoN6pWAcGAg

💝 https://youtu.be/9Mt8E-P9IUE

💝 https://youtu.be/-JfDXOdy2ek

👑 TikTok: www.TikTok.com/@MarvinaSims1

👑 Twitter: Twitter.com/@WEWIN_Queendom

👑 LinkedIn: https://www.linkedin.com/feed/

👑 🏰 Clubhouse: https://www.clubhouse.com/club/wewin-queendom?

Your follow helps us build a stronger community to Empower Women!

Everyone needs a little help sometimes.

Suicide:
CALL: 1-800-273-8255
OR
TEXT: HELLO TO 741741

Domestic Violence:
CALL: 1-800-799-7233
OR
TEXT: SUPPORT TO 741741

Bullying:
1-800-420-1479
OR
TEXT: HOME TO 741741

Self Harm:
CALL: 1-800-366-8288
OR
TEXT: CONNECT TO 741741

LGBTQ+:
CALL: 1-866-488-7386
OR
TEXT: START TO 678678

Sexual Assault:
CALL: 1-800-656-4673
OR
TEXT: HOME TO 741741

Abortion:
CALL: 1-866-439-4253
OR
TEXT: HELPLINE TO 313131

Pregnancy Infant & Child loss:
CALL: 1-800-944-4773
OR
TEXT: HELLO TO 741741

Grief:
CALL: 1-800-445-4808
OR
TEXT: CARE TO 839863

Eating Disorders:
CALL: 1-800-931-2237
OR
TEXT: NEDA TO 741741

For more hotlines & resources visit:
GRIEFRESOURCENETWORK.COM

Mental Health:
CALL: 1-800-950-6264
OR
TEXT: NAMI TO 741741

WORKS CITED

Evans, Patricia. *Controlling People: How to Recognize, Understand, and Deal with People Who Try to Control You.* Adams Media, 2002.

Sources for STACKED CELL HOLES

[1]Daisy Dukes are form-fitting denim short shorts first popularized by actress Catherine Bach in the late 1970s. Bach played the role of Daisy Duke, the beautiful cousin of lead characters Bo and Luke Duke in the television series *Dukes of Hazzard.* https://www.wisegeek.com/what-are-daisy-dukes.htm

Choldin, Harvey M. *Chicago Housing Authority: Rockwell Gardens Projects Demolishing.* The Electronic Encyclopedia of Chicago. 2005. https://chicagoganghistory.com/housing-project/rockwell-gardens/

Hunt, D. Bradford. *Blueprint for Disaster: The Unraveling of Chicago Public Housing.* 2009.

Popkin, S., Gwiasda, V., Rosenbaum, D., Amendolia, J., Johnson, W., Olson, L. *Combatting Crime in Public House: A Qualitative and Quantitative Longitudinal Analysis of the Chicago Housing Authority's Anti-Drug Initiative.* Justice Quarterly, 3 Sep. 1999, Vol. 16 No. 3, 520-57.

Seligman, Amanda. East Garfield Park. 2004, www.encyclopedia.chicagohistory.org/pages/404.html

West, Gerald and Patricia Krizmis. "Life in a Project: Hell Holes Stacked on Top of Each Other." Chicago Tribune (1963-Current File). ProQuest Historical Newspaper: Chicago Tribune. 29 Nov. 1971.

The Wam-O-Slip-N-Slide and the Water Wiggle! Wham-O TV Commercial: https://www.youtube.com/watch?v=JvGH8n0_-pw&feature=youtu.be

Jailhouse Rock – Elvis Presley https://www.youtube.com/watch?v=gj0Rz-uP4Mk

Walter Cronkite, CBS News Special Report, Resignation of President Richard M. Nixon, 8 Aug. 1974. https://www.bing.com/videos/search?q=Walter+Cronkite+Resignation+of+Richard+M.+Nixon&view=detail&mid=B14741D1F80EEDB6086DB14741D1F80EEDB6086D&FORM=VIRE

Sources for NUMBING OUT

[1]Inside the theme song: M*A*S*H's "Suicide is Painless" by Johnny Mandel, MTV Staff, August 14, 2018 www.metv.com

[2]SweeTarts is sweet and sour candies invented by Jeff Sousa in 1962. Using the same recipe as the already popular Pixy Stix and Lik-M-Aid products, in response to parents' requests for a less-messy candy. https://en.wikipedia.org/wiki/SweeTarts

[3]Theme song intro of the 1980s series Cheers "Where Everybody Knows Your Name" written by Gary Portnoy https://en.wikipedia.org/wiki/Where_Everybody_Knows_Your_Name (YouTube)

www.ingramcontent.com/pod-product-compliance
Lightning Source LLC
Chambersburg PA
CBHW071945190726
48293CB00004B/1351